Tips & Traps
for Building Decks,
Patios, and Porches

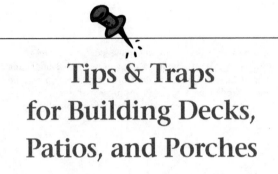

Tips & Traps
for Building Decks,
Patios, and Porches

R. Dodge Woodson

McGRAW-HILL

New York   Chicago   San Francisco   Lisbon   London
Madrid   Mexico City   Milan   New Delhi   San Juan
Seoul   Singapore   Sydney   Toronto

The McGraw·Hill Companies

Cataloging-in-Publication Data is on file with the Library of Congress

1 2 3 4 5 6 7 8 9 0   DOC/DOC   0 1 0 9 8 7 6 5 4

ISBN 0-07-145042-4

The sponsoring editor for this book was Cary Sullivan and the production supervisor was Pamela A. Pelton. It was set in Garamond by Lone Wolf Enterprises, Ltd. The art director for the cover was Handel Low.

Printed and bound by RR Donnelley.

Interior clipart images courtesy of www.clipart.com.

McGraw-Hill books are available at special quantity discounts to use as premiums and sales promotions, or for use in corporate training programs. For more information, please write to the Director of Special Sales, McGraw-Hill Professional, Two Penn Plaza, New York, NY 10121-2298. Or contact your local bookstore.

 This book is printed on recycled, acid-free paper containing a minimum of 50% recycled, de-inked fiber.

I dedicate this book to Adam, Afton, and all of the people who have helped me over the years.

Contents

About the Author

R. Dodge Woodson is a career contractor with over 30 years of experience in the trades. He owns and operates The Masters Group, Inc. Woodson specializes in residential projects ranging from home improvements to home construction.

Introduction

Improving your home is usually a good investment when the work is done correctly and within a viable budget. Adding a deck, porch, or patio to your home will provide exterior recreational space and should add to the value of your home. Some homeowners elect to do their own projects, but many of them change their minds once they get a feel for what is involved with the time and effort. What looks like simple work can be both complicated and exhausting to complete in a professional manner.

If you are not going to do the work yourself, how can you improve your odds of finding the best contractor for the job? Should you hire a self-employed individual or a company who has established work crews? Will the contractor you select require a pre-construction deposit payment that you may never see again? The process of finding and contracting the right worker or company can be almost as difficult as doing the physical construction yourself. But, this book can change the level of difficulty associated with contractor negotiations.

R. Dodge Woodson, a career contractor with 30 years of experience, and Mike Conroy remove the mystery of how to work with contractors in a way to save yourself time, money, and inconvenience. There is no reason to go it alone on your project. Don't suffer the pain of learning from mistakes that you can avoid. Let Woodson and Conroy show you how they deal successfully with subcontractors on a daily basis. Their years of experience are invaluable to any homeowner seeking the help of contractors and subcontractors.

Take a few moments to review the table of contents. Thumb through the pages and take note of the tip boxes that will pinpoint procedures at a glance. Look at the numerous forms that will give you direction in the process of finding, evaluating, and contracting workers. This book should be considered one of your most valuable tools when having home improvements added to your property.

1

Should You Be Your Own Contractor for Home Improvements?

There are projects in life where you can use your talents and experience and others you would never even consider trying. A friend knows of your culinary prowess and asks you to make her wedding cake; no problem. The den needs more shelves, and in a matter of minutes you have completed the task. It's simply a matter of the right tools for the job and a little knowledge of the basics.

Yet, suggest remodeling your house or making home improvements and there are usually just two reactions, "Are you out of your mind!" and "We're not talking a few shelves here, we're talking major work. I can't do that." Just as with the shelf installation, you will find you have experience in remodeling you never knew existed. Organization, patience, and basic product knowledge are all essential elements to any home improvement project. You need only to examine your qualifications and decide if you have the skills required to run your own job. If not, investigate choosing the right person or people for the project. Should you coordinate the work or hire a general contractor? This question will require a lot of thought. The wrong decision can be very expensive and frustrating. Being your own general contractor can save you a lot of money. It can also cost you more than paying professionals to do the work. Before jumping into a quick decision, consider all the factors. A little time spent now can save a lot of time and money later.

There are several types of qualified contractors available. They range from major corporations to individual, one-man firms. The trick is locating and choosing the right contractor for your job. Remodeling is often a complicated process and requires special talents. Matching your needs to the contractor's ability is mandatory for a successful job. There is much more to being a general contractor than hiring a few subcontractors and scheduling the work. If the role of a general contractor was easy, it wouldn't be such a lucrative business.

Remodeling and home improvements vary dramatically from new construction. You will encounter problems and unexpected complications not found in new construction. Many homeowners look immediately to what they perceive to be simple aspects of a home improvement project. They think they can do much of the work themselves to save money. Don't be fooled! Even a simple alteration, like changing the bathroom faucet, can be laborious and plagued with problems. The supply lines could break or crimp, or there may be no water cut-off valves to the faucet. Entire sink tops have been known to break during a routine faucet replacement. There is a difference

Many homeowners discredit the idea of doing work themselves, but contemplate acting as their own general contractor. This involves more details to consider than just saving a few dollars. It is only with the right personality and ability that these savings become a significant factor. The potential savings are very tempting. The lure of keeping up to 30 percent from coordinating your own project has a strong influence on many consumers. Some homeowners are well suited to the task. If you fall into this category, you are fortunate. Your savings overall should average about 20 percent.

between coordinating the changes made by professionals and acting as a tradesman. Only consider doing work yourself in areas were you have specific experience. Keep in mind, if you are using a plumber to replace your bathroom fixtures, you will not save much installing the faucets yourself.

MONEY TO BE SAVED

The percentage of money that can be saved by being your own contractor is based on the total value of the job, not the cost of the work. This is an important detail. There is a sizable difference between the retail value of the improvement and the cost to make the improvement. Your profit will be based on the retail value. An estimated job cost indicates the anticipated cost of completing the job. The value is based on the appraised worth of the completed project.

When you hire a contractor to do home repairs for you, expect the contractor to make a minimum profit of 20 percent of the improvement value. Let's assume the value of your job is $30,000. The general contractor wants this same appraised value for his work. Acting as your own contractor, the job should only cost around $24,000. You could do a lot with the $6,000 savings. However, if you prefer hiring out the work, you should be checking to make sure that your contractor is not pocketing more than 20 percent of the total value of the improvement.

It is best to engage a professional appraiser to ascertain the value of large home improvements. A general rule of thumb is, cost plus 20 percent equals value. When you examine your anticipated savings, use retail values.

The responsibilities of a general contractor are tedious and can be a losing proposition. If the job is not handled properly, money and time will be lost. Before becoming a contractor, consider the consequences carefully.

Questions to Ask Yourself Before Becoming Your Own Contractor

- Will you have time to arrange for blueprints and specifications?

- Will you be available to supervise the work while it's being done?

- Is special insurance needed to protect you from liability?

- Do you have a basic knowledge of the kind of work you are considering, such as the steps involved to replace your bathtub?

- These are just a small example of the questions to be answered.

More Questions To Ask Yourself

- Do you have time to be your own general contractor?

- How much time is required?

- Are you going to be available during the normal working hours?

- Will you be able to make phone calls in the evenings?

- Are you able to leave work for a few hours if necessary?

- Can you afford to take off from work to tend to your home fires?

As a general contractor, you will be responsible for coordinating all work and budgeting. Without extremely good organizational skills and a basic knowledge of construction, you can lose more than you save.

SUBCONTRACTORS

Unfortunately, many subcontractors may not be very dependable. This creates problems for even the most experienced general contractors. These subs can be difficult to motivate, even for a professional with years of experience. As a home-owner, with only one remodeling job, you are likely to find subcontractors difficult (but not impossible) to control. The demands on your personal time must be carefully evaluated. You will spend hours running the job. Much of this time will conflict with your standard work schedule. If you are not at your remodeling job, you don't know if the subs showed up. You won't know about their absence until the evening. By then, you have lost a whole day of production. Your night will be spent calling all the other contractors, because their work will have to be rescheduled. Every trade depends on another trade. When one is out of step, they are all thrown off schedule.

MATERIAL DELIVERIES

Material deliveries come during business hours. Are you able to confirm deliveries from work? Unfortunately, the numerous daytime phone calls required to coordinate your project will be a distraction. Will your job allow enough flexibility to make these calls? They must be made, how will you accomplish the chore? It may be wiser to hire a professional management team or general contractor.

> Your regular job can suffer when your time is divided by supervising the home improvement project. Weigh your sacrifices, and don't risk losing your full-time job. The remodeling savings won't justify becoming unemployed. You will need to devote a large portion of your spare time to the home improvement project. Determine what your time is worth.

What will you do when your materials don't arrive? The subcontractors are there, but they have no material to work with. The subcontractors are going to request additional compensation for time lost due to a lack of materials. Material acquisition is the general contractor's responsibility. If you fail to get materials on the job, it will cost you big money. Suppliers are a problem, even for the pros. Can you handle them? What will you do when the cabinets, which were going to take six weeks for delivery, are late?

Your first reaction will be one of anger. You will want to tell the supplier to take a hike, but where can you get the cabinets any quicker? This type of problem is common. You've waited six weeks already. If you change suppliers, you will have to wait even longer. If you rely on the existing supplier, who now promises delivery in two weeks, will you wait two weeks and still not have the cabinets? The supplier did not meet their first delivery date, what guarantee do you have that they will meet this one?

These are tough decisions, even for a seasoned professional. Most contractors will gamble on the two-week delivery. Sometimes they lose and the cabinets still don't show up. The contractor is a prisoner of the supplier. Making the right decision is based on unknown factors. How can you trust suppliers who do not keep their commitments? This dilemma can keep you up at night. All you can do is decide based on experience or gut reaction. There are ways to protect yourself from delivery catastrophes. The point being made here is that these are the types of events involved with supervising your home improvement project.

What Will You Have To Do?

- As a general contractor, you are responsible for everything.

- You will need to produce cost estimates as part of the planning stage for your project.

- If you are applying for financing, you need to know if the lender will accept your estimates.

- Does the lender's policies allow a homeowner to be the general contractor?

- Will the code enforcement office issue you the proper permits?
- Where will you obtain plans and specifications?
- Do you have the available cash to front the expenses of the job?
- Will your experience be adequate to keep the subcontractors honest?
- How much control will you have over the subcontractors?

ESTIMATING

Cost estimating can be tedious. You can read books in an attempt to learn estimating techniques. Some books will tell you what to expect for the cost of various projects. These books can be a good idea, but they are expensive. Their expense must be weighed against the money and time they can save you. A few flaws exist with estimating books. For example, the time requirements and estimates given are not universally accurate. Many of the books base their cost figures on union wages. Very few residential jobs are done by union members. Trade wages can differ by more than five dollars per hour. This factor alone can make a dramatic difference on a large job.

Another fault found in many of these books is the geographical cost differences. Prices in California cannot be compared to the prices in Florida. Maine contractors and suppliers will charge different prices than the same vendors in Virginia. Some companies, like the R.S. Means Company, Inc. of Kingston, Massachusetts, publish a variety of books which include a City Cost Index to allow for geographical differences. The *Means Home Improvement Cost Guide,* and the *Means Repair and Remodeling Cost Data* book are specifically geared to home improvement projects. These types of books will provide you with a rough idea of what to expect. The books are good for use as guides and reference material. They are an excellent educational tool in learning the steps of construction or remodeling. Certainly, they have value to the uninformed consumer, but don't accept the figures for costs until you adjust for your geographical location.

Firm quotes from suppliers and contractors provide the best way to estimate your intended job cost. There will be much less room for error in your estimate.

There is an easier way to get accurate figures. This approach won't erode your valuable time and the figures obtained will be reliable. This is the method I used when I first became a general contractor. Firm quotes from suppliers and contractors provide the best way to estimate your intended job cost. There will be much less room for error in your estimate. These quotes will guarantee many of your expenses. Written quotes can even be obtained through the mail. This is a simple process, but you need to know specifically what to ask for. If you already know what you want, you are way ahead of the game. If you don't, do some research. This is where those estimating books can be of the most help.

SPECIFICATIONS

When you embark on a remodeling or improvement project, you will need to invest enough time to create specifications. The specifications must be very specific. Read books, talk to suppliers, look at advertisements. All of this will prepare you for creating clear specifications. When you know exactly what you want, contact the bidders. When you ask a plumber for the price to install your bathroom, the plumber will require details. What brand of fixtures do you want? Do you want copper water distribution pipe, or PEX tubing? If you decide on copper, do you prefer type "M," "L," or "K."? Would you like schedule 40, PVC piping for your DWV system, or do you prefer ABS? What grade fixtures do you want? Fixture options include Competitive, Builder Grade, Standard, and Top-of-the-Line. Will you want your bathtub to be fiberglass, acrylic, steel, or cast iron? How much do you want to spend on your faucets?

Lavatory faucets start at less than twenty dollars and can cost more that $2,000.

Is a 1.6 gallon, water saver toilet suitable for your job? The principal is a good one, but will one and a half gallons of water be sufficient to flush the toilet with your old pipes? Should you have a china lavatory or a cultured marble top? Do you want an oak veneer vanity or a solid wood cabinet? Does it really make a difference? Will particle board delaminate in the bathroom moisture? Had enough of the question bombardment? All right, you get the overall idea.

These are only a few of the decisions a general contractor must make. The questions are determined by your individual situation. For example, should you invest in a temperature control shower valve? It is a very good safety feature if there are young children or elderly members in your family. If you have back problems or elder family members, an 18-inch toilet is a wise investment. Of course, unless you are clairvoyant, you will not know all the questions to ask. Remodeling and home improvement is a step-by-step process. First you will come up with an idea of the changes you want to make. Then you will start to choose the accessories to make those changes a reality. How will you know what questions to ask? The same way a general contractor does. List all of your requirements and desires. Then contact vendors of those products. It can be as simple as asking a plumbing supplier, "Is there any way to protect our children against accidental scalding?".

You will be amazed at the variety and usage of products available. For example, spas and whirlpools offer unlimited opportunities. You can spend $2,000 or $6,000. What is the difference between a spa and a whirlpool? Most people don't know, but you are about to learn. The big difference is that spas are designed to hold water indefinitely. You fill them, treat the water with chemicals, and they are constantly ready for your enjoyment. Whirlpool tubs are meant to be filled with water each time you use them. This can be an expensive form of relaxation. Consider the cost of producing hot water to fill the whirlpool. Many units hold ninety gallons of water, or more. In most residential situations, you will empty your water heater each time the whirlpool is filled. Heating this volume of water consumes a lot of expensive energy. Whirlpools are less expensive, but spas offer more benefits. While on this subject, it is worth mentioning that certain products, such as bubble bath oils, may not be recommended for use with whirlpools and spas. Check the manufacturer's recommendations before putting any additives into your bath or spa water.

If you buy an expensive carpet with an inferior pad, you are making a mistake.

Now let's make you a carpeting expert. Carpeting is an easy job for the homeowner to subcontract, right? Not unless you know the keys to the floor covering industry. If you buy an expensive carpet, with an inferior pad, you are making a mistake. The pad is the most important part of your floor covering. An inexpensive carpet on a quality pad will last much longer than an expensive carpet on a poor pad. Do you know how to recognize a good carpet or pad? Ask the carpet representative to show you the difference in the available products.

Have them put four sample pads on a floor along with four different grades of carpet. Lay the carpet samples on each pad. Now, with heavy soled shoes, walk on the carpet. Which carpet was the quickest to eliminate your footprints? Make a note of the carpet and have the salesperson move the carpets to different pads. Try the test again. Did the same carpet win? I doubt it. The proof is in the pad. This procedure allows you to determine the difference between carpets and their pads. You can easily evaluate your best value with this procedure.

What knowledge do you have of heating systems? Can you determine the BTUs required to heat your living space? What type of heat will best meet your requirements? You can choose between heat pumps, boilers with tankless coils, electric heat, and forced hot air units. The standard energy sources include, electricity, oil, natural gas, and LP gas. Here is a suggestion. Contact your power and utility companies. Many power companies offer programs designed to save energy and increase your savings. You may find they can answer many of your questions regarding properly heating your improved home. Is natural gas available in you neighborhood? If possible, should you heat your hot water with your home heating system? Will it supply an adequate volume of hot water? Will your existing electrical service accommodate your new improvements? If the utility company doesn't have the answer, try asking the local codes enforcement office.

Other questions are not as easily answered. How many coats of mud will your new drywall require? Do you need to prime or seal your surfaces before painting? What thickness of insulation should you use in your new space? These are all important questions. As a general contractor, you must be able to answer them. Your only hope, if you can't find answers to these questions, is honest subcontractors. Honest subcontractors can be hard to find.

It is unlikely, as a homeowner, you will be fully versed in answering these technical questions. Professional general contractors have many advantages over the average homeowner. Experienced general contractors have dealt with the majority of problems commonly encountered. They know which products are commonly used versus which ones are required. General contractors use subcontractors on a regular basis. They know their subcontractor's faults. Due to the future work available from the contractor, subcontractors will respond quickly to the request of the general. Experienced general contractors know how to handle problems that arise on a daily basis. Successful generals have endured the test of time. They have paid the dues for their experience.

> As a homeowner, you run the risk of losing money as a general contractor. If events go as planned, you will save a bundle. If they don't, you'll lose your shirt. Average homeowners are better off working with a licensed general contractor.

YOUR ABILITIES

How will you determine your abilities? Don't let potential savings taint your judgement. You must address your project objectively. If after thorough evaluation, you feel qualified to tackle the job, do it. Consider all the repercussions before making a final decision; it may be more cost effective to hire a professional remodeling contractor. Your time has value, determine this value and compare it to the cost of a good contractor. At first glance, being a contractor looks easy. This encourages many carpenters to go into the remodeling business to fulfill their dreams of untold riches. Homeowners fall into the same trap. General contracting is not easy, it is hard work and requires special abilities.

home improvement projects rarely go as planned; the ability to make sound judgement calls is paramount. Don't force yourself into a failing situation which could doom your entire project for the sake of a few dollars.

General contracting is not a fountain of financial freedom. The profession is plagued with uncontrollable circumstances. General contractors are dependent on subcontractors. If the subs don't do their job, the general cannot do his. This is a frustrating and helpless feeling. A homeowner only has one job to offer the subcontractor. If a scheduling conflict arises, the homeowner loses. Subcontractors almost always respond to the people providing their primary income. This is rarely the homeowner. Subcontractors are dependent on general contractors. When a general calls, the sub will respond. This can require stalling a homeowner's job. They must look at their long-term income. A homeowner only has one job to offer, the general contractor has many profitable jobs during the year. As a self-contractor, you will be faced with this problem.

General contractors are in business to make your life easier. You pay them 20 percent of the job's value to take care of the problems. They coordinate everything. When you have a problem or a question, you deal with the general contractor. All of your problems are handled through one source, and this is a strong advantage. Simply contacting all the subcontractors involved in a change order is a time consuming process. Almost any changes made will affect several subcontractors. For instance, the decision to move your vanity farther down the wall will result in numerous phone calls. The first call will be to the plumber. Then, the electrical contractor will need to be contacted to move lights and outlets. The carpenter may need to adjust for the changes.

This simple vanity relocation may affect your ceramic tile design. When the decision is made after drywall is hung, you'll have to contact the drywall contractor. There may even be a conflict with your heating system's location. This example shows the effect of a so-called simple change. For each sub-contractor involved, you will spend a lot of time on the phone and on the job site. These situations drain your personal time. A general contractor will handle all these changes after just one phone call from you

The general contractor will coordinate all material deliveries. As a self-contractor, would you be able to handle improper material shipments? What will

If your time is valuable, a general contractor is a good investment.

happen when the material you were promised for Tuesday still isn't on site by Friday? This means down-time for your craftsmen. They will want reimbursement for lost production time or may leave to do another job. If you are the general contractor, it is your responsibility to provide for and coordinate their work. Once they have left your job, it is unlikely they will come back until their next contract is complete. If you have a full-time, regular job, how will you get these problems resolved? Suppliers are hard to deal with and can be very undependable. They are notorious for broken promises. Paying plumbers to stand around, while you locate their missing material will cost you a small fortune. You can count on this problem arising, there is no way to avoid it. By hiring a general contractor, these headaches become their problem.

Subcontractors can ruin your production schedule. If your heating contractor does not show up, you will have to reschedule your other subs. When the insulator lets you down, you have to rearrange your drywall contractor and painter. Everything that goes wrong creates a chain effect. With a general, the problem still exists, but you don't have to deal with it personally. If you follow the rules you learn in this book, you will have written clauses in the contract to insure your job is completed in a timely manner. The general contractor is the one losing sleep over scheduling problems, not you.

Subcontractors can ruin your production schedule.

Paying for the work is another advantage to a general contractor. General contractors will frequently bill you. For large jobs this could be on a monthly basis. On the other hand, subcontractors will want payment upon completion of their work. This can be a problem if you are financing the job. Lenders will expect you to pay tradesmen and suppliers before advancing a loan disbursement. Financing presents its own challenges, and is an entirely separate consideration.

What other factors do you need to think about before deciding to be your own general contractor? There is the consideration of protecting yourself and your home. Will you need additional insurance? Acting as your own general contractor may not be covered under your existing insurance. General contractors carry liability insurance to protect you and your property. You should ask for evidence of this insurance before signing any contracts with a general. There are many potential risks which make liability insurance compulsory. What happens if a carpenter drives a nail through your water distribution pipe? Your house floods! Who is responsible for the damage repair? How will you handle an electrician falling through your ceiling? It wouldn't be the first time someone was working in the attic and lost their footing. When using a general contractor, the contractor is responsible to you for these damages. Without a general, will your homeowner's insurance protect you?

Before making a final decision on who will run your project, read the rest of this book. The following chapters hold a wealth of information. Your decision on who should handle the contracting of the job will be easy to make when you are fully informed. It's tempting to try to get by without professional management. I encourage you to take advantage of the opportunity, if you are qualified. Evaluate what you learn from this book and make educated decisions. Take the Contractor Quiz, at the end of this chapter, as a tool in evaluating your potential as a general contractor. The time you spend researching your options will be well rewarded.

> Investigate your liability insurance needs before acting as a general contractor. You don't want to be on the losing end of a lawsuit, there is no money saved if that occurs.

The information here will not protect you from all of the pitfalls of remodeling and home improvements. It would be impossible to anticipate all the potential problems. Even after thirty years as an active remodeler, plumbing contractor and general contractor, I still learn something new with many jobs. While I can't protect you, I can prepare you for the journey into having work done on your home. Your project will run much smoother with the proper knowledge. This knowledge will benefit you as a consumer or a contractor.

For the following questions, rate your answers on a scale of one to ten. On the scale, one is very weak or not at all. Ten is very strong or a definite yes. For example, if the question was,"Do you have a full-time job?," this is how you would answer. Indicate the numeral 10 for a full-time job. Use the number 5 for a part-time job and use number 1 if you don't have a job. If the question was, "Can you make quick, accurate decisions?," this is how you would answer. If you feel strongly that you can, enter the number 10. If you are unsure of your ability, enter a number between 1 and 5. If you have average decision making skills, use the number 5.

ARE YOU READY TO BE YOUR OWN CONTRACTOR?

1. Rate your ability to supervise your project
    during the day.   0   5   10

2. Do you have a full time job?   0   5   10

3. Do you enjoy working with people?   0   5   10

4. Do you have strong leadership ability?   0   5   10

5. Are you comfortable around strangers?   0   5   10

6. How often do you believe what you are told?   0   5   10

7. Do you act on impulse without thought?   0   5   10

8. Are you allergic to dust?   0   5   10

9. Do loud, repetitive noises bother you?   0   5   10

10. Does your regular job require you to
    manage people?   0   5   10

11. Do you enjoy talking on the phone?   0   5   10

12. How willing are you to work nights,
    scheduling subs?   0   5   10

13. How easily are you intimidated by people?   0   5   10

14. Do you have a shy personality?   0   5   10

15. Can you make confident decisions?   0   5   10

16. How much will you research
    remodeling principles?   0   5   10

17. Are you sensitive to fumes and odors?   0   5   10

18. Are you good with numbers?   0   5   10

19. Do you have a creative mind?   0   5   10

ARE YOU READY TO BE YOUR OWN CONTRACTOR? (continued)

20. Can you visualize items from a
    written description?   0   5   10

21. Do you have strong self discipline?   0   5   10

22. Do you fluster easily?   0   5   10

23. Do problems cause you extreme stress?   0   5   10

24. Rate your organizational skills.   0   5   10

25. Are you vulnerable to sales pitches?   0   5   10

26. Do you have time to find subcontractors?   0   5   10

27. Do you enjoy negotiating for the best price?   0   5   10

28. Is your checkbook balanced today?   0   5   10

29. Do you utilize a household budget?   0   5   10

30. Do you feel qualified to control irate
    subcontractors?   0   5   10

31. Do you have strong self confidence?   0   5   10

32. Do you lose your temper easily?   0   5   10

33. Can you react quickly to unexpected events?   0   5   10

34. Can you make personal calls from work?   0   5   10

35. Do you buy bargains, even when you don't
    need the items?   0   5   10

36. Is your time financially valuable?   0   5   10

37. Will you be available to meet code
    enforcement inspectors?   0   5   10

38. Do you have a gambler's personality?   0   5   10

(continues)

ARE YOU READY TO BE YOUR OWN CONTRACTOR? (continued)

39.	Can you be assertive?	o 5 10
40.	Do you enjoy reading technical reports and articles?	o 5 10
41.	Do you retain information you read?	o 5 10
42.	Do you pay attention to small details?	o 5 10
43.	Do you know people who work in the trades?	o 5 10
44.	Do you trust your judgement?	o 5 10
45.	Can you keep accurate, written records?	o 5 10
46.	Are you able to do more than one task at a time?	o 5 10
47.	How well can you prioritize your day and your duties?	o 5 10
48.	Do you feel qualified to coordinate your project?	o 5 10
49.	Can you stand to watch your house being torn apart?	o 5 10
50.	Are you capable of staying out of the way of the workers?	o 5 10

Add your total score and compare it to the ranges given below to get an idea of your ability to act as the general contractor.

SCORES AND OPTIONS

If your score is 186 or less, seriously consider hiring a professional general contractor. Your answers indicate a weakness to perform the functions of a general contractor. This score may mean you do not have the right personality for the job. Technical points can be learned, but personalities are hard to change. You may be able to accomplish the task if you do extensive research and address your weak points. Keep your quiz answers in mind as you read this book. The book will help you to clearly identify the areas you need to address. For homeowners in this scoring range, hiring a professional is the safest route to take. Before trying to coordinate your own job, read this book and evaluate what you learn. Chances are, you will decide to hire a professional to manage your job. There is nothing wrong with this. Not all people are designed to run construction crews and jobs.

If your score is between 186 and 280, you have the ability to learn how to get the job done. Most of the areas you need to work on are remodeling related and can be learned. In this mid-range, you should be able to read enough to attempt the job at hand. Your score indicates some areas of weakness. As you complete this book, note the areas of weakness in your knowledge. Spend the time needed to strengthen these areas. With enough preliminary planning, you should be able to run your own job.

If you scored between 280 and 375, you are a natural. With the right research, you can be an excellent general contractor. The higher your score, the better qualified you are. If you scored near 375, all you will need to do is polish your knowledge of the trades; you already possess the basic qualities of a good general contractor. Even with a high score, you still have a lot to learn. Complete this book and, when you feel completely comfortable with your abilities, move ahead. You will be ready to command your construction crews and save money.

2

Screening and
Selecting Contractors

So you want a new deck, patio, or porch. If you're one of the lucky few, not only do you know exactly what you want, but you have an uncle who's the best deck builder in town. But, if you're like most people, you just know you want some living space in the yard. You may have an idea of what you want, but that's the extent of it. Now you have to go from wanting to getting - and you need help.

But where do you turn, and who can you trust? Will your contractor be up-front and honest? Do you need a contractor? Can you believe your neighbor who just spent six months building his deck? How do you know you won't get taken advantage of?

If these thoughts are racing through your head, you're the norm, not the exception. Most people get a little apprehensive when they're considering a home improvement project. It can be a daunting task. There's so much to consider that people tend to get overwhelmed. Which is O.K.; a little fear can be self-preserving. But to proceed correctly, and to keep your fear from taking over, you'll have to consider many things.

This chapter will cover the information you need to screen and select a qualified contractor.

Contractor selection is one of the most important decisions you'll make on your project. It's important to choose a contractor that fits your needs, not just your budget. There are many considerations to be made, one of the least is price. I'll walk you through the process and list important topics to cover so you can make a wise decision.

> It's important to choose a contractor that fits your needs, not just your budget.

SEARCHING FOR THE PERFECT CONTRACTOR

Searching for a contractor can be a lot like searching for a good pair of shoes; you're going to have to try several on to find a good fit. Your first job will be to locate the several you want to 'try on'. There are many ways to find them.

I'm going to point you in the right direction, and steer you away from the wrong ones. Remember, you're just trying them on for now. Don't limit yourself to only contractors who have _____. Now fill in the blank with: a large yellow page ad; new trucks; small crews; fancy stationary; etc.

You'll want to contact several different 'types' of contractors to find the one that fits your needs the best. If you limit your search with narrow criteria, you may miss the contractor that's just right for you and your project.

Initial Contact

Find phone numbers for several contractors you want to talk to. Find them by talking to friends, the yellow pages, ads on the sides of trucks, yard signs, radio/newspaper advertisements, or any other way. Your goal should be several to start with, and then begin narrowing the field from there. Use different means. Don't pull them all from a single source, such as the yellow pages.

FIGURE 2-1
Locate the contractors you want to contact in a variety of places.

By limiting your search criteria, you limit your contractor pool. The best way to locate contractors is through word-of-mouth advertising. By talking to your friends, neighbors, and co-workers who've had work done, you should be able to get a personal reference for several contractors. If someone you trust has had work done by a certain contractor, who better to give you a reference for them?

The worst way to find a contractor is to flip open the phone book and call the three with the biggest ads. While this is the method preferred by many people, it is way too limiting on your potential contractor pool. Remember, to find the contractor that's best for you, you'll want to pull your list from as many sources as possible.

Once you have a list of 4 - 6 potential contractors, call them. Set a pre-bid meeting at your house to look at your situation and discuss possibilities. Let them know you'll be looking for their input and using it to help decide exactly what you want them to estimate. Explain that, after your pre-bid meeting, you'll call them with a final decision on what you want them to bid. Always use caution when letting someone in your home. Check their identification and never let anyone in when you're alone.

Don't pull from a single source, such as the yellow pages.

A pre-bid meeting is your initial face-to-face contact with your potential contractors. You want to get their input and get an initial feel for who they are and how they conduct themselves. Explain your basic ideas and options, and ask if they feel qualified to handle the task. At the meeting the contractor should give you his input and look at where you want to add your outdoor living space.

Set a specific time with each contractor for the pre-bid meeting. I always try and schedule contractors one after the other. I want short enough meetings so I don't waste my whole day waiting for them, but long enough so I don't get them lined up waiting on each other to finish. 30 to 45 minutes is a nice amount of time to sit down and discuss your plans with each potential contractor. Allow at least fifteen minutes for time to reflect on each visit after it's over, but before the next contractor arrives. Depending on your personality - how much you like to talk - you should schedule your appointments 45 minutes to an hour apart.

By scheduling this way you can listen to each one's ideas separately, and get a feel for who knows what. If three of five potential contractors point out an important issue that needs to be handled, and the other two miss it completely, you'll know which three to call for written estimates. For example, you have five contractors scheduled in 45-minute increments between 10 AM and 1:45 PM. The first, second, and third contractors point out that to put the screen room where you want it, you'll have to move a bedroom window - the window just happens to be where the screen room wall will meet the house. Obviously, moving a window will require time and materials, both of which cost money. If your other two potential bidders miss this point, they'll fail to put this cost in your bid. This will cause major problems down the road. Someone has to pay for the work. Now is the time to determine who's to be responsible for it.

This oversight on your potential contractors' part is a warning of how things may work if you hire them. Scratch the two who missed the required work from your list, and move forward.

> 30 to 45 minutes is a nice amount of time to sit down and discuss your plans with each potential contractor. Allow at least fifteen minutes for time to reflect on each visit after it's over, but before the next contractor arrives.

There are many important things to watch for when you first begin contacting and meeting with a new contractor. These items may seem small, but they're great indicators of how they'll take care of you in the future. Jot them down so you can mark which contractors live up to these standards.

1. Does he promptly return your phone calls? You shouldn't have to wait more than one business day to get a return call. If they won't call you when you're a

potential customer, do you think they'll call if you become an angry one?

2. When at your home, do they answer their cell phone? I know it would be considered polite to turn it off, but in today's world, that just isn't practical. Consider yourself on the other end of the call. If you're the customer on the other end of the line, and you have a question or concern with your project, you'd want him to answer. You'll want him to be accessible if his crews are working on your house. Ask him how, and who, you'll need to contact in case of emergency on your project? If it's not him directly, is there a foreman or project leader who'll be responsible for your job? And how will you contact him/her?

3. Is the contractor taking notes while he's talking to you about your project? Is he taking measurements? Has he looked at all areas of the house that'll be affected? If a contractor glances quickly over your project before he bids it, how much attention to detail will he put in while he's working on it? How can he bid your new cabinets if he never pulls out a tape measure to see how long they need to be?

4. Is he in a hurry? Is he trying to rush you? If he won't spend time with you now, while he's trying to sell you his services, do you think he'll spend time with you after he's sold you his project?

5. Is he answering your technical questions? Is he knowledgeable about the work he's trying to sell you? I'm not saying he should know everything, but he should know a considerable amount. Be leery if he can't answer your questions. Decks, patios, and porches are pretty straight-forward objects to construct. Any contractor with moderate experience should be very knowledgeable about these subjects.

6. Ask if the contractor and his crew have completed similar projects before? Do they do this kind of work on a

regular basis? If not, what makes him think he can do it now? Does he have enough other experience to give him the knowledge he needs to finish your project?

7. Is the contractor currently working? If not, why not? If it's the peak of the season and your contractor's not busy, he should have a very good explanation. Otherwise, I'd stick to the ones that are actually working.

Consider each contractor's behavior and answers. You should begin to get a feeling about each of them. At this point, you want to continue gaining knowledge of each contractor so you can narrow the field. The goal is to narrow your search to a minimum of three to provide you with a written estimate.

Each contractor should provide some insight into your plans, uses, and maybe even some ideas that you haven't thought of. Make sure you ask plenty of your own questions. You shouldn't be concerned with insurance, references, licensing, etc., at least not yet. These issues will be covered later. Right now you want to continue to add to your gut feeling about each contractor. Make a list of points to discuss, and take notes while talking with each contractor (consider using the back of the piece of paper you used before to jot down your questions). Be sure and cover the following points with each one:

1. Explain your basic needs and ideas again. Ask for their suggestions to meet those needs. For example, if your primary concern is having a safe area for your toddler to play on, he may suggest a patio instead of a deck. Patios are built right on the ground so there's no place like stairs for your young one to fall off. I know this sounds redundant, but you'll be digesting a large amount of information and it's easy to forget the basics. It's an old carpenter's adage that says "Measure twice, cut once." Use this philosophy when it comes to the basics of your project; cover them twice.

2. Ask for an idea of price. Don't push for it and don't expect great accuracy; but some contractors can give

you a quick idea of a square-foot price so you can get a ballpark idea of cost. For a simple deck or patio, they should be able to wing an approximate cost, especially if they do this work regularly.

3. Ask if they do their own work, have their own crews, or if they subcontract their work. If they subcontract their work, how long have their subs been working for them? Will you be able to obtain references for the particular subcontractor who will complete your project? Will you be able to see an example of this particular sub's work? Checking on another one of his subcontractors, who won't be doing your project, does you no good. In this case you are actually hiring two contractors, the general and the sub - so you need to check them both out.

4. If they don't do their own work, find out who'll be responsible for your project; and how you'll be able to contact them. Do they carry cell phones? Are they radio-dispatched? You should always have a way to contact the person in charge of your project.

5. Ask who'll be responsible for required building permits. If your potential contractor refuses to get the permit, call your permit office and see if there's a reason why. Permit offices won't let contractors who aren't in good standing obtain permits. You can find this information by contacting your local building and zoning department. The number is available in your phone book in the government listings.

6. Ask about the final touches such as clean up, removal of debris, landscaping, etc.

Remember there's no such thing as a dumb question. If you obtain conflicting answers from your potential contractors, ask the one who's there currently to clarify his answer. After he's done so, tell him what the other contractor said. Write down his clarification and response so you can do some research later to determine if one of your contractors is mistaken. Remember, there's more than one way to skin a cat. Just because two contractors will handle things differently, doesn't necessarily mean one of them is handling it wrong.

FINAL CHECKS AND SELECTION

You've held the pre-bid meeting and now it's time to decide which contractors you want to estimate your project. Choose at least three to work up estimates. But how do you know who's O.K.? How do you know these guys aren't just good salesmen? Who can you check with to make sure you're in good hands? What else should you check? These are the typical questions running through homeowners' minds, and the final part of this chapter will address them for you.

I'll outline the sources you can use to 'check up on' your contractors. There are many things you should check before getting an estimate and much more so before signing a contract with anybody. Most people don't bother with the effort to make these checks, and many end up wishing they had. Take the time to screen your contractors thoroughly to avoid making the wrong hiring decision and regretting it later.

Insurance

All contractors need insurance. They should be able to provide proof of the different types they carry. At a minimum they should have general liability and worker's compensation insurance. Don't hire a contractor who can't provide proof of these types of insurance.

There are no federal regulations that pertain to the amount of insurance a contractor must carry. According to my friend and insurance agent, Monte Rogers, "Insurance requirements vary state to state. The minimum policy my company (American Family Insurance) will write is 300/600." What Monte means when he says "300/600" is a general liability policy that covers liability up to $300,000 per person and $600,000 per occurrence. These amounts are clearly stated and you should check these amounts when you're reviewing your contractor's policy.

Monte says 99% of the general liability policies he writes are for at least $500,000/$1,000,000. He says people feel much more comfortable when a contractor can say he has a million dollars of coverage.

Your contractor should also carry worker's compensation insurance on his employees. Worker's compensation covers employees when they get hurt on the job. This insurance is very crucial. If a worker gets hurt on your project, and the contractor does not have coverage, you can be held liable.

A contractor can carry additional coverage in the form of an Excess Liability policy, commonly called an umbrella policy. This coverage extends beyond the limits of his general liability insurance. For example, if your contractor has a general liability policy for $500,000/$1,000,000 and an umbrella policy of $1,000,000, the two policies combine for a total coverage of $2,000,000.

Use the following checklist to insure your contractor, and therefore you, are properly covered:

- **General Liability.** Check the amount of coverage and the policy effective and expiration dates. A fair amount of coverage will be at least $500,000 per person and $1,000,000 per occurrence. The effective dates should encompass the entire time frame of your project - from the start date to completion.

- **Worker's Compensation.** This insurance is critical if the contractor has any employees. Make sure the policy is in force and that the workers are covered for the type of work they are performing.

- **Excess Liability, commonly an Umbrella.** This policy is a bonus. It's not necessary, but does provide extra coverage.

ACORD™ CERTIFICATE OF LIABILITY INSURANCE

	DATE
	08/20/2002

PRODUCER	THIS CERTIFICATE IS ISSUED AS A MATTER OF INFORMATION ONLY AND CONFERS NO RIGHTS UPON THE CERTIFICATE HOLDER. THIS CERTIFICATE DOES NOT AMEND, EXTEND OR ALTER THE COVERAGE AFFORDED BY THE POLICIES BELOW.
Agency One Insurance Services 500 W MAIN ST RECEIVED	
DECATUR IL 62522- AUG 2 2 2002	**INSURERS AFFORDING COVERAGE**
INSURED	INSURER A: GRINNELL MUTUAL
NEIGHBORHOOD	INSURER B:
RENEWAL	INSURER C:
	INSURER D:
Decatur IL 62521-0000	INSURER E:

COVERAGES

THE POLICIES OF INSURANCE LISTED BELOW HAVE BEEN ISSUED TO THE INSURED NAMED ABOVE FOR THE POLICY PERIOD INDICATED. NOTWITHSTANDING ANY REQUIREMENT, TERM OR CONDITION OF ANY CONTRACT OR OTHER DOCUMENT WITH RESPECT TO WHICH THIS CERTIFICATE MAY BE ISSUED OR MAY PERTAIN, THE INSURANCE AFFORDED BY THE POLICIES DESCRIBED HEREIN IS SUBJECT TO ALL THE TERMS, EXCLUSIONS AND CONDITIONS OF SUCH POLICIES. AGGREGATE LIMITS SHOWN MAY HAVE BEEN REDUCED BY PAID CLAIMS.

INSR LTR	TYPE OF INSURANCE	POLICY NUMBER	POLICY EFFECTIVE DATE (MM/DD/YY)	POLICY EXPIRATION DATE (MM/DD/YY)	LIMITS	
A	**GENERAL LIABILITY**		/ /	/ /	EACH OCCURRENCE	$ 1,000,000
	X COMMERCIAL GENERAL LIABILITY				FIRE DAMAGE (Any one fire)	$ 1,000,000
	CLAIMS MADE [X] OCCUR	0000106782			MED EXP (Any one person)	$ 5,000
			/ /	/ /	PERSONAL & ADV INJURY	$ 1,000,000
					GENERAL AGGREGATE	$ 2,000,000
	GEN'L AGGREGATE LIMIT APPLIES PER:				PRODUCTS - COMP/OP AGG	$ 2,000,000
	POLICY [ ] PRO-JECT [ ] LOC		/ /	/ /		
A	**AUTOMOBILE LIABILITY**	0000106787	07/05/2002	07/05/2003	COMBINED SINGLE LIMIT (Ea accident)	$ 1,000,000
	X ANY AUTO					
	ALL OWNED AUTOS		/ /	/ /	BODILY INJURY (Per person)	$
	SCHEDULED AUTOS					
	HIRED AUTOS		/ /	/ /	BODILY INJURY (Per accident)	$
	NON-OWNED AUTOS					
			/ /	/ /	PROPERTY DAMAGE (Per accident)	$
	GARAGE LIABILITY				AUTO ONLY - EA ACCIDENT	$
	ANY AUTO				OTHER THAN EA ACC	$
					AUTO ONLY: AGG	$
	EXCESS LIABILITY		/ /	/ /	EACH OCCURRENCE	$
	OCCUR [ ] CLAIMS MADE				AGGREGATE	$
						$
	DEDUCTIBLE		/ /	/ /		$
	RETENTION $					$
A	**WORKERS COMPENSATION AND EMPLOYERS' LIABILITY**	0000106782	07/05/2002	07/05/2003	WC STATU-TORY LIMITS [ ] OTH-ER	
			07/05/2002	07/05/2003	E.L. EACH ACCIDENT	$ 500,000
					E.L. DISEASE - EA EMPLOYEE	$ 500,000
					E.L. DISEASE - POLICY LIMIT	$ 500,000
	OTHER		/ /	/ /		

DESCRIPTION OF OPERATIONS/LOCATIONS/VEHICLES/EXCLUSIONS ADDED BY ENDORSEMENT/SPECIAL PROVISIONS
CERTIFICATE HOLDER IS ADDITIONAL INSURED SUBJECT TO FORM GMGL1805

CERTIFICATE HOLDER	ADDITIONAL INSURED; INSURER LETTER:	CANCELLATION
ATTN MIKE CONROY CITY OF DECATUR 1 GARY ANDERSON PLAZA DECATUR IL 62523-		SHOULD ANY OF THE ABOVE DESCRIBED POLICIES BE CANCELLED BEFORE THE EXPIRATION DATE THEREOF, THE ISSUING INSURER WILL ENDEAVOR TO MAIL **30** DAYS WRITTEN NOTICE TO THE CERTIFICATE HOLDER NAMED TO THE LEFT, BUT FAILURE TO DO SO SHALL IMPOSE NO OBLIGATION OR LIABILITY OF ANY KIND UPON THE INSURER, ITS AGENTS OR REPRESENTATIVES. AUTHORIZED REPRESENTATIVE

ACORD 25-S (7/97)   © ACORD CORPORATION 1988
INS025S (9910).01   ELECTRONIC LASER FORMS, INC. - (800)327-0545   Page 1 of 2

FIGURE 2-2
This Certificate of Liability Insurance shows the contractor's coverage limits.

- **Check ALL the contractors' insurance.** You have to check the insurance for all contractors who'll be working on your project. This includes all subcontractors. Don't just check the general contractor's insurance and assume you'll be covered; check them all!

References

The use, or uselessness, of this issue can be debated. After all, what contractor in his right mind would give you someone who's unhappy with him as a reference? But I recommend you check these anyway. You may be surprised at what people will tell you over the phone; your contractor may be surprised as well. People are a lot more apt to let their frustrations out when the person they're talking about isn't listening.

Have your contractor provide you with names and contact information of three customers he's completed work for recently. Preferably he can provide names of people who've had work done that's similar to yours. If he's building you a deck, ask for the names of customers that he's built decks for. While any reference will give you insight into how he conducts business overall, a targeted reference let's you know how well he does on jobs like yours.

Contact these references and ask if they had any problems with the contractor or his crew? Was the work completed on time and to their satisfaction? Did the project come in on budget? Would they hire the contractor again? Did the worker's clean up after themselves, or did they leave a mess? Have they needed any warranty work done on the project? If so, was it handled promptly and courteously?

You'll get a real feel for how the contractor conducts his business from his past customers. Sure he's going to do his best to provide the names of satisfied customers, but next I'll show you how to see if any of his disgruntled customers have spoken up.

Visiting a Jobsite

Have your contractor provide you with an address(s) where he or his crews are currently working. If you can, get the address of a project that's similar to your own. Get his permission to visit the site at your convenience.

Visit the site when you can. Make sure the workers are present and stop by for a short visit. Be mindful that they're working on someone's house, but have a look around. Pay attention to what's being done and how the workers conduct themselves. Is the jobsite a disaster? Keep in mind that it's a construction site, but it shouldn't look like a tornado just went through either. Are the workers courteous? Are they being careful of the home they're working on? Are they wearing shirts with profanity or other distasteful items on them? Do they have their music up so loud you can't hear yourself think? Would you want this crew working on your home? Remember they may be at your house soon.

Licenses

In your area are contractors supposed to be licensed? Does your contractor have the required license to complete your project? If not, is he planning on hiring someone with the proper license? These are all questions you should ask before signing a contract.

To determine what licenses are required in your area, contact your local building and zoning department. The phone number for this agency will be listed in the government pages of your local phone book. If there's no listing for this office, contact the municipal offices and inquire who handles building inspections.

Once you contact the person or office in charge of inspections, inquire what trades require licensing. Do they require all contractors to be licensed - or just certain contractors?

In my area only certain contractors have to be licensed to conduct certain types of work. Plumbers, electricians, heating contractors, and roofers all have to have licenses, but general contractors don't need one. For example, a general contractor can build an entire house - but the workers, or subcontractors, who complete the plumbing, electrical, and heating have to have licenses. Check the regulations in your area to determine which licenses are needed for your particular project, then check to see that your contractor has the proper licensing.

Check Your Local Better Business Bureau (BBB) and Chamber of Commerce

It's always a good idea to check with these agencies to see if your contractor is in good standing or if they've had complaints registered against them. You can find the phone numbers for these agencies in your local phone book. Check in the business listings section.

When you contact these agencies, keep in mind that no one can make everyone happy. A single complaint wouldn't scare me away from a contractor if everything else checked out O.K. However, I know of an agency that had logged 142 complaints against a single contractor and the number was still rising! Obviously, you wouldn't want to hire a contractor with multiple complaints.

The number one cause of consumer complaints for years has been contractor problems. If people in your community have had problems with your pick, you want to know now, before you sign a contract.

SUMMARY

To sum up the chapter, you want to check out your contractor before you hire him. While you're checking on him, make sure you follow these guidelines:

- Start by contacting several contractors. Set up a pre-bid meeting with each potential contractor.

- Ask each contractor many questions and get a feel for how they conduct their business.

- Pay close attention to how your potential contractor treats his current customers.

- Check references, insurance, a current jobsite and the BBB before obtaining estimates.

Hiring a reliable contractor is one of the major necessities needed to complete your project successfully. By following the advice in this chapter, you'll be able to effectively screen your list of contractors to the three or more that you want to provide written estimates.

3

Avoiding Zoning Problems

I f you've ever had dealt with zoning issues, you know why problems are best avoided. Never has the proverb, "An ounce of prevention is worth a pound of cure." been more true than in this situation. If you do your research, you can avoid very costly trouble by following the guidelines set forth in your local zoning ordinance.

If you haven't had to deal with them before, you may know very little about them. However, most communities have some form of them. They can dictate where you can put structures on your property, what types are allowed, and how large the structure can be.

If you don't follow the ordinance, you can be ordered by a court of law to correct the problem and gain compliance. If you fail to correct the problem and gain compliance, you can be held in contempt of court and maybe even thrown in jail. But this kind of action very rarely happens. Most problems can be solved by other means. If you read this chapter and follow the advice contained within, you'll have the best of possible scenarios; avoiding all issues BEFORE they become problems. You can achieve this by simply being informed.

If you don't follow the ordinance, you can be ordered by a court of law to correct the problem and gain compliance. If you fail to correct the problem and gain compliance, you can be held in contempt of court and maybe even thrown in jail.

WHERE CAN I FIND ZONING INFORMATION?

The path to finding the information needed to avoid trouble starts with knowledge you may already have. This knowledge will depend on factors such as your vocation, your involvement in the community, and usually your past involvement (or run-in) with a zoning issue. Don't feel bad about lack of experience with zoning. Zoning ordinances are foreign to many people just like you. If you're not a builder, developer, or work in your local government, you may never have even considered them.

Zoning Boundaries and What They Mean to You

We all live within certain boundaries. We live in a community - that's in a county - that's in a state - that's in a country. There are unseen boundaries all around us. We live in a certain zip code, a certain school district, and whether we've known it before now, or not, a certain zoning ordinance boundary. Before you can figure out what zoning ordinance you fall under, we have to start with your address.

Don't assume that because your address says a certain city that you're automatically under that city's ordinances. I have a Decatur, Illinois address, but I don't fall under Decatur's zoning ordinances.

Lots of people are in a similar situation with their properties. I have a Decatur address, but my property is in Long Creek Township. I have a Mt. Zion phone number and I live in the Mt. Zion School district, but I fall in the Macon County real estate tax area. With all these different boundaries for one property, it's no wonder people get confused!

To find your proper area, you can visit your local Recorder of Deeds Office. The Recorder will have a record of what district you fall in. They will consult a map, called a plat, which will show what district you reside in.

When you visit the Recorder's Office, the person at the office will be able to help you find your property on the plat. They'll also be able to help you locate the boundaries for which township, village, or city your property lies in.

> To find your proper area, you can visit your local Recorder of Deeds Office.

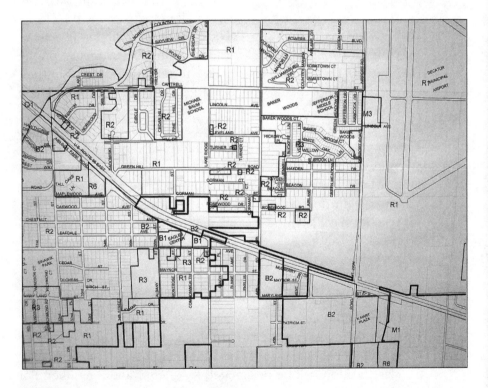

FIGURE 3-1
A plat, like the one shown, is a map that shows the boundaries and easements of your property.

Most cities and townships are incorporated and the boundary lines are clearly defined. Don't assume that you are in, or out of, a certain township or city because of your neighbor's status. The lines don't always run straight. Just because three properties are in a row doesn't mean they're all within the same boundary. As in my example, one property can be in a city's boundaries, while its neighboring properties are located in another community.

> Don't assume that you are in, or out of, a certain township or city because of your neighbor's status.

Another option, which may be quicker and easier than traveling to the Recorder's Office, would be to pick up the phone and call your local government offices. Look in the government listings of your local phone book for the Planning Department's phone number. This office may be able to tell you if you're in their district, or not. Start with the offices of the city in which you know, or think, you live in.

This phone call may save you a trip and some time by getting you an answer in a hurry. Unfortunately, you never know who you're talking to when you're on the phone. You may get a secretary or someone in the wrong department. If you get the wrong information, it won't cause problems for anyone but you. If I have any doubt at all, I go to the Recorder's Office and check for myself.

Your Zoning Classification and What It Means

Once you've determined what district you're in, you'll need to determine what your property's zoning classification is before you lose contact with whoever is helping you. Your zoning classification will be designated by a letter and a number. For example, if you're in a primarily residential district, you'll have a designator for your zoning classification such as R-1. The R designates a residential classification while the number designates how restrictive the allowed uses are.

The lower the number is in your designator, the more restrictive the ordinance is on what and where you can build. My zoning ordinance has five zoning classifications pertaining to residential areas alone. This doesn't even consider classifications for business, agriculture, or industrial uses. And the permitted uses can vary widely. It's important to find your designator so you can properly decipher your local ordinances. Once you've found the designator for your property, you can move on to the next step in planning your project for zoning compliance.

> If you're in a primarily residential district, you'll have a designator for your zoning classification such as R-1. The R designates a residential classification while the number designates how restrictive the allowed uses are.

A Copy of Your Local Ordinance

Now that you know what municipal boundary, and therefore what zoning ordinance, you fall under, and what your property is zoned, you have to find a copy of the ordinance so you can begin planning your project accordingly. You can obtain a copy from whatever municipality governs you, or you may be able to obtain a copy from your local library.

Your Local Government

To purchase a copy, you first have to find the offices of the government agency that's responsible for the ordinance. Consult your local phone book and make some phone calls before you run all over town trying to find the right office. I recommend you call and get the exact location where you need to go, and the hours of operation for the office. It's also wise to check the cost and the methods of payment they'll accept.

This process can require a few phone calls. Navigating through the myriad of government offices may take some time. You may have to contact several offices before anyone knows the information you need. Don't give up. Start with your local Building and Zoning Department. They should know, but you never know who's answering the phone.

Some offices' phone systems will transfer a call if the primary line for the office is busy. You may assume you're talking to the Zoning Department when you actually have a secretary from another office on the line. You have to persist until you find someone who can help you. Once you locate them, find out where you can obtain a copy of the ordinance.

Navigating through the myriad of government offices may take some time. You may have to contact several offices before anyone knows the information you need. Don't give up.

The Public Library

If you're like me and you want to save your money, visit your local library. They should have a copy of the ordinance on file for your review. You won't be able to take it home, but you can review it while you're there.

Before you visit your library, take the time to call your local Building and Zoning Department to determine when the ordinance was last ratified. Your library will invariably have some old copies on hand. If you design your project off of an old ordinance copy, and the guidelines within it, you may be asking for trouble. To avoid problems, make sure you're reviewing the most recent copy.

Visit the help desk at the library and ask where they keep the government publications, specifically the local zoning ordinance. Once you've located the section with the publications, locate your local ordinance. Check the date on the ordinance to insure you have the most recent copy, and therefore one that's currently being enforced. You should have obtained this information when you called your local Building and Zoning Department.

If you design your project off of an old ordinance copy, and the guidelines within it, you may be asking for trouble. To avoid problems, make sure you're reviewing the most recent copy.

FIGURE 3-2
Your local library should have a section of available local government publications including code books and zoning ordinances.

Take a pen and paper with you when you're reviewing the
ordinance to write down any and all pertinent information. But
what are you looking for? How do you know what pertains to
your situation? The next section in this chapter will answer
these questions for you.

HOW THE ZONING ORDINANCE
AFFECTS YOU

Deciphering your zoning ordinance can be confusing. But
once you know what you're

> The three issues you need to determine
> are whether your building will conform to
> the permitted uses, the permitted sizes,
> and the permitted setbacks for your zoning
> district.

looking for, you can find the answers to your questions and get on with your project. I'll break out the primary issues you need to cover to construct your outdoor living space without causing issues with your local officials.

There are three main points that need to be determined to insure your building conforms to your local ordinances. To find this information you'll need to navigate the table of contents of your newly found Zoning Ordinance. I'll point out what you're looking for and how to decipher the tables and information. I'll give you some examples to follow so you can wade through the mass of information and find what you need.

The three issues you need to determine are whether your building will conform to the permitted uses, the permitted sizes, and the permitted setbacks for your zoning district. Let's look at these three issues one at a time.

Permitted Uses

Open your copy of the Zoning ordinance for your district and locate the table of contents. Now scan down to the section that covers your particular zoning classification. For example, your property is zoned R-6. So you want to locate the section entitled R-6 - Multiple Dwelling District, or something similar. Then locate the page number it lists for this section and turn to that page.

In this section of the ordinance you'll find a subsection entitled Permitted Uses. Listed in this subsection will be all of the permitted uses for this district classification. If the use you are looking for is not included in the list, don't panic yet. You'll want to check the listing for lower zoning classifications to see if the use you desire is listed there. Some ordinances will print all permitted uses for all classifications, while others only print uses not included in lower zoning classifications. By this I mean that if the permitted use of two-family dwellings is permitted under a classification of R-5, it is permitted in the higher classification of R-6 as well, but may or may not be printed in the permitted uses for the R-6 classification. By scanning the uses of lower classifications, you may find your desired use and therefore know it is permitted.

If, on the other hand, you do not find your desired use, begin scanning the uses for higher zoning classifications. Scan the classifications from yours to the highest classification, or until you find the use you want listed, in the order they appear. For example, you want to operate a bed and breakfast out of your home, and you're adding on a patio for your guests to use. But the use of B and B is not permitted in your R-3 zoning district. By scanning forward to the next higher classification, R-5, you find you can operate your business with a special use permit.

Now you know you have a zoning problem and must get rezoned and get a special use permit to do what you want. At this point you'll need to do some intensive research with your local Planning Department to determine if you still want to move ahead with your project, or not.

But hopefully you've found the use you want, unlike my example above, and you can move on to the next compliance issue to insure you have no problems with your design and plans.

Height and Area Regulations

Now that you know your use is in compliance with the code, it's time to ensure you can build where you want and how big you want. I know, to some of us, it seems ridiculous that the "powers that be" can dictate not only how we use our buildings, but how big they can be and even where we put them on our property, but they can. And the time to make sure they'll be OK with what you're doing is now, not after construction is finished.

Once again, we must consult the zoning ordinance section that covers your particular zoning classification. Once there, find the subsection entitled Height and Area Regulations.

The dimensions you'll want to pay attention to are the minimum yard areas, number of stories, and maximum height. While the last two figures will not likely be a factor for an outdoor project such as a deck, patio, or porch, pay attention to them for future reference. Let's look at these restrictions one at a time.

- **Minimum yard areas.** This includes the minimum front, side, and rear yard areas. This is the amount of space you must allow from the boundary line of your lot when building a structure. For example, the minimum side yard area for your zoning classification is 10 feet. This means that no portion of your structure, or attachments to the structure, may extend closer than 10 feet to your property line on either side of your house. Let's look at a scenario to see if it complies with the 10-foot side yard setback. Let's say you have 20 feet measured from the house to your side lot line. You want to construct a covered porch around the side of the house that will be 12' deep. This will leave 8' between the porch and the lot line. This does not comply with the setback. To correct the situation, the porch will have to be shortened to 10' deep, or you would have to seek a variance. Talk to your local Building and Zoning Department to consider the possibility of a variance. This may or may not be a viable option available to you. I'll talk more on variances in the next section of the book.

- **Number of stories.** This number has no effect on most patios, decks, and porches, but may apply to your particular situation. Therefore, I wanted to discuss it briefly. If your plans include any structure that will have a roof, you'll want to insure you don't build more stories than your ordinance will allow. The allowable number will be available in your particular zoning classification and/or the Height and Area Regulations chart in your zoning ordinance.

Districts	Buildings Maximum Height		Yard Depths Minimum		Side Yard Width Minimum		Lot Size Minimum	
	Stories	Feet	Front Feet	Rear Feet	Either Feet	Aggregate Feet	Width in Feet	Area Per Family Square Feet
Residential								
R-1	2½	35	30	20	10	20	80	20,000
R-2	2½	35	25	16	8	16	60	9,000
R-3	2½	35	25	12	5	12	50	6,000
R-5	2½	35	25	12	5	12	50	5,000 1 unit 2,500 2 units
R-6	3	35	25	12	5	12	50	4,000 1 unit 2,500 2 units See Sec. IX.C >2 units
Office								
O-1	3	45	25	12	5	12	50	Same as R-6
Business								
B-1	2	35	25	0	5	10	0	6,500
B-2	3	45	25	0	5	10	0	10,000
B-3	2	35	30	25	50	0	0	20,000
B-4	12	150	0	0	0	0	0	200
Industrial								
M-1	10	125	25	0	5	10	0	6,500
M-2	10	125	25	0	0	0	0	10,000
M-3	See Special Regulations in Section XVIII.							

FIGURE 3-3
A Height and Area Chart from your local zoning ordinance outlines building restrictions for your area.

- **Maximum height.** As with the previous bulleted item, this may or may not pertain to your particular situation. This number will be listed with the maximum number of stories in your particular classification's section and/or the Height and Area Regulations chart in your zoning ordinance.

After reviewing the requirements of your local zoning ordinance, you should now know if your intended project will comply or not. If you're having difficulty understanding or interpreting anything from your ordinance, contact your local Building or Zoning Department for assistance. They will be able to answer your questions or point you in the right direction to insure compliance. The number for your local department will be in the government listings of your local phone book.

VARIANCES AND REZONING

Hopefully your research yielded the information you wanted, and your intended use meets all of your local zoning ordinance requirements. Then you can skip this section of the book. However, if your intended use does not meet with local requirements, you have two options to consider next. One is obtaining a variance; the other is to get rezoned. The process for the first option can sometimes be a simple matter of filling out a form and paying a fee, but sometimes the process for either solution can be almost impossible. The key is to know before you build, and try to correct the situation at that time before you begin. You don't want to find out after you've already built that what would have been a small issue is now a Goliath of a problem.

So, your project doesn't fit in the guidelines of your local ordinance. What do you do? First, don't panic! There are solutions, and I'll outline them for you. I'll discuss each one so you'll have a clear understanding of where to begin to solve your issues with the ordinance. As with most things that deal with government, there is a specific path you must follow to resolution. The journey becomes much easier when you know the path that leads to a successful end. Now let's look at both paths.

> If your intended use does not meet with local requirements, you have two options to consider next. One is obtaining a variance; the other is to get rezoned.

Variance - Can I Get One?

This is the question that needs answered - Is a variance even an option for you? But first let's discuss what a variance is. A variance is a written order from your local zoning official(s) allowing you to "break" the limits outlined in the ordinance. A common example is extending into the required setback. For example, in older neighborhoods, it's common to find garages built on or near the lot lines. They are built so close because they were erected before the zoning ordinance was drafted and adopted by your local municipality. But if you want to build a new garage, or rebuild your old one, you have to conform to the standards. In this case you may apply to your local zoning body for a variance to erect the garage closer to the lot lines than is allowed by the ordinance. If they agree, in writing, this is a variance. They are allowing you to bend the rules in this particular circumstance, and this particular circumstance only.

> In older neighborhoods, it's common to find garages built on or near the lot lines. They are built so close because they were erected before the zoning ordinance was drafted and adopted by your local municipality.

Now that we know what a variance is, let's look at how you apply for one. I say apply, because there is no guarantee that you'll get it. Typically, you have to fill out a form, pay a fee, and have your case reviewed by the local Zoning Board of Appeals. This process will take some time. How much time depends on when you apply and when your local board meets.

City of Decatur, Illinois
PETITION FOR VARIANCE

Zoning Board of Appeals
Economic and Urban Development Department
One Gary K. Anderson Plaza
Decatur, Illinois 62523-1196

424-2781
FAX 424-2728

SECTION ONE: PETITIONER / OWNER / REPRESENTATIVE INFORMATION

Petitioner						
Address						
City		State		Zip		
Telephone		Fax		E-mail		
Property Owner						
Address						
City		State		Zip		
Telephone		Fax		E-mail		
Representative						
Address						
City		State		Zip		
Telephone		Fax		E-mail		

SECTION TWO: SITE INFORMATION

Street Address	
Legal Description	

Present Zoning	R-1	R-2	R-3	R-5	R-6	Is this property a Planned Unit Development?
	B-1	B-2	B-3	B-4	O-1	☐ YES Approval Date: _____
	M-1	M-2	M-3	PMR-1		☐ NO

Please list all improvements on the site:	
Size of Tract	☐ SF ☐ AC

Page 1 of 2

(continues)

FIGURE 3-4
To receive a variance, you'll need to fill out a petition such as the one shown here.

SECTION THREE: REQUESTED ACTION			
Check One:	☐ Variation of Specified Site Requirements (e.g. setbacks)	☐ Variation of Parking & Loading Requirements	☐ Other - classification of use, off-street parking in an "R" zone, special circumstances, etc.
Description	*Please state the reason for exception, variation or appeal to the Zoning Board of Appeals. Be as specific as possible, detailing the circumstances that make an appeal necessary. Additional descr iption pages may be attached.*		

SECTION FOUR: ATTACHMENTS	
Description	*Please list any attachments and/or supporting documents below:*

Attachments to this petition should include a scaled sketch plan of your proposal showing property lines, lot dimensions, buildi ng dimensions, all buildings on the property, setbacks, requested changes in the requirements and other necessary information. Please label this sketch plan as "Exhibit A" and other supporting documents accordingly. Architectural or engineering drawings are preferred, but not required.

SECTION FIVE: CERTIFICATION	
	To be placed on the agenda of the regular meeting on the second Thursday of the month at 4:00 PM in the City Council Chamber, petition must be received on the first Thursday of the prior month. Petitioner or a representative must be present to make statements to the Board and to answer questions. Incomplete or erroneous petitions may delay items being heard by the Zoning Board of Appeals.
Petitioner's Signature	Date

NOTES:

1. Please forward this completed form and attachments to the Economic and Urban Development Department, Third Floor, Decatur Civic Center. A filing fee of **$150.00** is charged for all requests for property in the R-1, R-2, R-3 and R-5 districts, and **$250.00** for property in all other districts. Please make checks payable to the City of Decatur.

2. Signature of this petition grants permission to City staff to place a sign, indicating a request for zoning action, on the subject property at least 10 days prior to the Zoning Board of Appeals hearing. Said sign will be removed within 15 days of the Zoning Board hearing.

Page 2 of 2

FIGURE 3-4 *(continued)*
To receive a variance, you'll need to fill out a petition such as the one shown here.

The form you fill out is called a petition. Next you have to pay the appropriate fee to the appropriate governing body. The amount of time it takes to have your petition reviewed depends on when you submit it and when your board meets. My local Zoning Board of Appeals meets on the second Thursday of every month. However, the deadline for submitting petitions is the first Thursday of the preceding month. This means your request will sit for at least 5 weeks, and for as many as 9 weeks, before it is reviewed. Depending on how fast you want to start your project, this may or may not be a big factor. If time is of the essence, you may want to alter your plans to fit within the existing guidelines rather than trying to get a variance to fit your needs. But if you have the time, and completing the project as planned is important, by all means, stick to your guns and go for the variance.

If time is of the essence, you may want to alter your plans to fit within the existing guidelines rather than trying to get a variance to fit your needs.

Once your case goes before the review board, a decision will be made to grant or deny your request. The decision of the board is considered final. If you have to petition you local board, I hope the decision goes your way.

Rezoning - Is This for Me?

Some variances are easy to apply for and receive. However, rezoning may be another issue. Time frames and fees charged will all increase when compared to obtaining a variance. The initial petition will be similar but the similarities between the processes ends there.

Depending on the type of local government you have, your petition for rezoning may not go to the Zoning Board of Appeals, but before the elected officials. You will have to attend public hearings, have signs posting your desire for

	City of Decatur, Illinois
	PETITION FOR REZONING
	Petition before the Mayor, City Council and Members of the Plan Commission of Decatur, Illinois
	Economic and Urban Development Department
	One Gary K. Anderson Plaza 424-2793
	Decatur, Illinois 62523-1196 FAX 424-2728

Please Type

SECTION ONE: PETITIONER / OWNER / REPRESENTATIVE INFORMATION

Petitioner					
Address					
City		State		Zip	
Telephone		Fax		E-mail	
Property Owner					
Address					
City		State		Zip	
Telephone		Fax		E-mail	
Representative					
Address					
City		State		Zip	
Telephone		Fax		E-mail	

SECTION TWO: SITE INFORMATION

Street Address	
Legal Description	

Present Zoning	☐ R-1	☐ R-2	☐ R-3	☐ R-5	☐ R-6	Is this property a Planned Unit Development?
	☐ B-1	☐ B-2	☐ B-3	☐ B-4	☐ O-1	☐ YES Approval Date: _____
	☐ M-1	☐ M-2	☐ M-3	☐ PMR-1		☐ NO

Please list all improvements on the site:

Size of Tract		☐ SF ☐ AC	

SECTION THREE: REQUESTED ACTION

Rezone Property To:	☐ R-1	☐ R-2	☐ R-3	☐ R-5	☐ R-6	Will this property be a Planned Unit Development?
	☐ B-1	☐ B-2	☐ B-3	☐ B-4	☐ O-1	☐ YES
	☐ M-1	☐ M-2	☐ M-3	☐ PMR-1		☐ NO
Other:						

(continues)

FIGURE 3-5
The initial petition for rezoning is similar to the one needed for a variance, but the remaining process is vastly different.

Section Three Continued	
Purpose	Please state the purpose of the proposed rezoning.

SECTION FOUR: JUSTIFICATION

The petitioner submits to the City Plan Commission and City Council the following facts (additional pages may be attached):

SECTION FIVE: CERTIFICATION

	To be placed on the agenda of the regular meeting on the first Thursday of the month at 3:00 PM in the City Council Chambers, petition must be received on the first Thursday of the preceding month. Failure of the petitioner or the petitioner's representative to attend the Plan Commission hearing may result in items being tabled. Incomplete or erroneous petitions may delay items being heard by the Plan Commission.
Petitioner's Signature	**Date**

NOTES:

1. Please forward this completed form and attachments to the Economic and Urban Development Department, Third Floor, Decatur Civic Center. Please make checks payable to the City of Decatur. See Schedule "A" for fees.

2. Signature of this petition grants permission to City staff to place a sign, indicating a request for zoning action, on the subject property at least 10 days prior to the Decatur City Plan Commission hearing. Said sign will be removed within 15 days of final action by City Council.

3. In the event a petition for rezoning is denied by the Council, another petition for a change to the same district shall not be filed within a period of one year from the date of denial, except upon the initiation of the City Council or the City Plan Commission after showing a change of circumstances which would warrant a renewal.

4. All petitions before the Decatur City Plan Commission are reviewed through the Development Technical Review (DTR) Process. Please consult the DTR Brochure for information related to this process.

Rev. 2 - 4/01

OFFICE USE ONLY	
Date Filed	
By	

Page 2 of 2

FIGURE 3-5 *(Continued)*
The initial petition for rezoning is similar to the one needed for a variance, but the remaining process is vastly different.

rezoning on the property, and attend meetings to answer questions regarding any opposition to your request.

You will be required to take an active role in rezoning. The work does not end once you fill out your petition and pay your fee. You will have to convince the officials that rezoning your property for your intended use will be good for your neighborhood, and the community as a whole. This may, or may not, be easily done.

Opposition by neighbors and/or local business people can and will kill your petition in a hurry. Most communities take rezoning seriously and don't consider rezoning property at the drop of a hat. You may have a fight on your hands. However, if you're prepared for this, property does get rezoned. If you want it bad enough, anything can happen. Fill out your forms, pay your fees, and go for it!

MY PROJECT CAN'T BE A NUISANCE — CAN IT?

Can simply doing construction be considered a nuisance in some communities? In a word: YES. The key factors are how and when you do it. I know it sounds unbelievable to some of us, but it's sad and true. To determine whether you'll cause a nuisance by renovating your home, consult your local Building and Zoning Department to see where you can find what governs construction in your area. In my area it's the City code.

My local government sets allowable hours of construction and states that no refuse may be placed on the ground. What does this mean to you? It means you should check with your contractor to insure he plans to abide by the local rules. You may be thinking that if the contractor breaks the rules it's his problem, but this may not be the case. Usually, the homeowner is the one cited when a violation occurs. The problem is that in some communities, the penalties for violations can be stiff - a possible fine of up to $500 for each day the violation

10. **GARBAGE ON PREMISES**. No owner or occupant of any premises within the City of

Decatur shall deposit or cause or permit to be deposited, or leave or permit to remain after receiving

notice, any garbage, debris or other waste on said premises except as elsewhere provided for the

collection of same by a licensed garbage hauler.

(AMENDED, Ordinance No. 2004-77, September 20, 2004)

11. **HOURS OF CONSTRUCTION**. The erection, including excavation, demolition,

alteration or repair of any building in any "R" or "O-1" zone as established by the Zoning Ordinance of

the City of Decatur, or within one hundred (100) feet of any part of said zones, is hereby prohibited

except between the hours of 7:00 a.m. and 6:00 p.m. except in case of necessity for public safety.

FIGURE 3-6
These rules govern hours of construction and construction refuse in my city.
What governs construction in yours?

To determine whether you'll cause a nuisance by renovating your home, consult your local Building and Zoning Department to see where you can find what governs construction in your area.

exists! With possible penalties so high, it's a good idea to check your local code and stick to the set guidelines.

Don't get upset worrying over possible fines though. Avoiding problems is simple, once you know what the rules are. And you're going to find out what they are before you begin.

SUMMARY

In this chapter we discussed the issues you need to address to avoid zoning problems. To recap, check all items on the list below to insure you comply with all local regulations:

- Insure in which jurisdictions and boundaries your property lies.
- Locate a copy of your local zoning ordinance.
- Determine the zoning classification of your property.
- Check permitted uses, height and area regulations.
- Apply for a variance or rezoning if necessary.
- Check to insure compliance to nuisance regulations.
- Proceed with project.

If you'll take the time to research and check the information from the above list, you'll save yourself some potentially large headaches before, during, and after your project. Some folks subscribe to the notion that it's easier to get forgiveness than permission. And while this may hold true in minor aspects of life, don't take this attitude with your home. The biggest investment of your life deserves more respect than that. Check the rules, comply with them, and you'll avoid problems with your project.

4

Avoiding Violations of Covenants and Deed Restrictions

Troubles arising from covenants and deed restrictions can not only be upsetting, they can be very costly. Ask me, I know from experience. The trouble, as with most written "guidelines" we must follow, is interpretation. What I read and interpret the language of a covenant or deed restriction to say may not be what someone else reads and interprets. Therefore there's room for disagreement, and when two or more people disagree, the potential for problems exists. The potential for problems is not good and should be eliminated if possible.

In an ideal world, there would be no disagreements, no lawyers, and no need for courts of law. However, we all know this won't happen in our world, at least not on this side of the grave. So what do you do? You take the necessary steps to protect yourself, your home, and your project.

But where do you start? At this point, you may not even know what a covenant or restriction is. You may even be asking how they can affect you and your project. As bewildering as it sounds, it's not complicated to understand or to discover what restrictions are on your property. First I'll explain what covenants and deed restrictions are, and then I'll explain how to find out what they mean to you and your project.

Some of the information included in this chapter will be a rehash of information from the last chapter. If you've read the last chapter, you may be able to skip some of the information in this one. If however, you did not read the last chapter for whatever reason, you'll want to read this one in full. The information included is vital if you are to avoid problems that may arise from the issues covered. Read it thoroughly, take the steps necessary to uncover the restrictions for your property, and apply them for trouble-free execution of your project.

When two or more people disagree, the potential for problems exists. The potential for problems is not good and should be eliminated if possible.

WHERE DO I BEGIN?

The path to finding the information needed to avoid trouble starts with knowledge you may already have. As stated before, your vocation, your involvement in the community, and usually your past involvement (or run in) with a restrictive issue are all factors. Don't feel bad if you've never had to work with covenants or deed restrictions before, or if you didn't even know they existed. These issues are foreign to many people. After all, if you're not a builder, developer, or local government official, you may never have had a cause to even consider them.

Covenants in Subdivisions and What They Mean to You

Covenants and restrictions are rules outlined by a developer that dictate what you can and can't do in their subdivision. These rules are set down on paper to accomplish many things. The idea is to insure that all properties in a subdivision are relatively the same. Not in style necessarily, but in size, amenities, and value. They are prescribed by the developer of the land.

The developer wants to insure the value of his building lots so he prescribes what kind of houses can be built in his subdivision and what they can have in the yard, and even what types of materials can be used.

Imagine a subdivision that is half-full of million-dollar houses and half-empty. Then imagine someone coming along and building a fifty-thousand dollar house on one of the remaining lots. People who build and live in million-dollar houses do not want to live next to a fifty-thousand dollar "shack". Once the "shack" (as the neighbors would see it) is built, the remaining lots of the subdivision have just gone down in value considerably. So, to protect his investment and that of the current lot owners, the developer sets in place covenants and restrictions to keep the structures and uses of the property similar to what they want, rather than leave it up to the individual lot owners to police themselves.

Depending on what your position is, you may view covenants and restrictions as good things that protect everyone in the subdivision, or as silly rules that shouldn't be enforced. Either way they're there to stay, and they have to be dealt with.

Covenants and restrictions can enforce many issues. Consider the following list which sets forth some examples of what they can control. However, do not consider this list as all inclusive, because it is not:

- Square footage. One of the most common restrictions is square footage. You are required to build a house of a certain minimum size for inclusion.

- Brick or stone. Often, a minimum amount of brick or stone is required on the front of houses in subdivisions.

- Plant requirements. Some subdivisions require you to plant certain kinds and numbers of plants and/or trees.

- Vehicle storage. Boats, inoperable or damaged cars, motorcycles, and RV's are often prohibited in driveways of more expensive subdivisions.

- Chain link and/or wooden privacy fencing. The type and size of allowable fencing is often dictated in restrictions.

- Outbuilding size and style. Often certain types of outbuildings are prohibited and or restricted to size in subdivisions.

- Pools, patio coverings and landscaping. All of these items can be regulated by the covenants and restrictions of your subdivision.

The idea is to insure that all properties in a subdivision are relatively the same. Not in style necessarily, but in size, amenities, and value.

- Outdoor pets and/or livestock. Newer subdivisions may even limit the quantity and types of pets and animals you may keep on your property.

FIGURE 4-1
Covenants and restrictions can dictate what type of fencing is allowed and how tall it can be. Check yours before beginning your project.

The previous list is just a sampling of what can be restricted on your property by your subdivision's covenants and restrictions. It's easy to see why it's important to find a copy of yours and insure that you follow the guidelines set forth in them to avoid problems. Violating the rules and having to gain compliance can not only be troublesome and time-consuming, it can be very costly as well. Read on to learn how to obtain a copy of your covenants and restrictions and how to interpret the information contained in them.

OBTAINING A COPY OF YOUR COVENANTS AND RESTRICTIONS

If you're informed, lucky, or have had a run-in with them, you may have a copy of the covenants and restrictions for your property lying around. However, if you're like most of us, you'll have to go searching for a copy. I'll outline the process for obtaining a copy in the next few paragraphs. The process can be easy and free, or it can take a little effort and some of your hard-earned cash. Where you live and how readily accessible certain parties are will determine which category you fall in. Let's discuss the easy ways first.

The Easy Way

You can obtain a copy of your covenants and restrictions from many places. The first two places should be easy and free. Let's talk quickly about these two and I'll hope in advance that you have luck with them.

The Chairman of the Architectural Control Committee

If you know who the chairman of the architectural control committee is and how to contact them, you're in luck. If you don't, you have a Catch 22 on your hands. You need to be able to contact the chairman to obtain a copy of the restrictions, but you don't know who the chairman is WITHOUT a copy of the restrictions! Sorry. Let's just say you do know how to contact

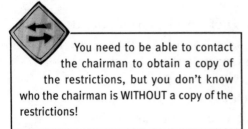

You need to be able to contact the chairman to obtain a copy of the restrictions, but you don't know who the chairman is WITHOUT a copy of the restrictions!

this person. If you do, make contact and ask for a copy of the covenants and restrictions for your subdivision. If you don't, stay calm. There still may be an easy way to get a hold of a copy.

A Friend or Neighbor from Your Subdivision

If you know (and don't assume you know - know you know, I'll explain why in later in this paragraph) that your friend or neighbor lives in your subdivision, ask them if they have a copy of the covenants and restrictions or if they know who is in charge of the architectural control committee. If they do on either count, your work is almost done and should be easy to complete. If not, keep reading and I'll show you how to obtain a copy the hard way.

The Hard Way

If you didn't already have a copy, and the easy ways failed you, you'll be reading this section of my book. I'm sorry. But don't panic. With a little leg work and phone calls, you should be able to obtain a copy of your covenants and restrictions in short order. I'll start by explaining some boundary issues. Some of this is a recap from the previous chapter, so if you've read it, you can skim the information here as it may be a review for you. However, if you didn't have a reason to read Chapter 3, you'll want to read this section very carefully.

Don't I Fall in the Same Boundaries As My Neighbor?

We all live in certain boundaries. We live in a community - that's in a county - that's in a state - that's in a country. There are unseen boundaries all around us. We live in a certain zip code, a certain school district, and whether we've known it before now or not, a certain subdivision. Before you can figure out what subdivision your property is in, we have to start with your address.

Don't assume that because your address says a certain city that you're automatically in that city's boundaries. I have a Decatur, Illinois address, but don't live in the City's borders.

Lot's of people are in a similar situation with their properties as I am. I have a Decatur address, but my property is in Long Creek Township. I have a Mt. Zion phone number and I live in the Mt. Zion School district, but I fall in the Macon County real estate tax area. With all these different boundaries for one property, it's no wonder people get confused.

To find what subdivision you reside in, you can visit your local Recorder of Deeds Office. The Recorder will have a record of what subdivision you're in; or better put, they'll have a map, called a plat, that will show what subdivision you reside in.

> One property can be in a particular subdivision while its neighboring properties fall outside the boundaries.

When you visit the Recorder's Office, the person at the office will be able to help you find your property on the plat. They'll also be able to help you locate the boundaries for which township, village, or city your property lies in. But most importantly, for this chapter, they'll help you figure out what subdivision your property is in.

Subdivision boundary lines are clearly defined. Don't assume that you are in, or out of, a certain subdivision because of your neighbor's status. Just because three properties are in a row doesn't mean they're all in the same subdivision. One property can be in a particular subdivision while its neighboring properties fall outside the boundaries.

Another option, which may be quicker and easier than traveling to the Recorder's Office, would be to pick up the phone and call your local office. Look in the government listings of your local phone book for the phone number of the

Recorder of Deeds office. This office may be able to tell you what subdivision your property lies in. Start with the office that governs the city in which you know, or think, you live in.

This phone call may save you a trip and some time by getting you an answer in a hurry. Unfortunately, you never know who you're talking to when you're on the phone. You may get a secretary or someone in the wrong department. If you get the wrong information, it won't cause problems for anyone but you. If you have any doubt at all, go to the Recorder's Office and check the information yourself.

If, however, you get someone who is knowledgeable and helpful, try and get the information you need. If they can tell you what subdivision you're in, ask for a copy of the covenants and restrictions for the subdivision. Ask them to fax, or mail, you a copy. This will be possible if there is no fee involved. If you have to pay a fee, you'll have to submit a formal request by mail with payment, or visit the office personally and pay the fee to obtain a copy of your covenants and restrictions.

READING AND DECIPHERING COVENANTS AND RESTRICTIONS

Once you have a copy of the covenants and restrictions for your subdivision, you have to be able to decipher what they say and apply that to your situation. Most covenants and restrictions read like legal documents and should be regarded as such. As I've stated before, violating them can be time consuming and costly. I know from experience. While this was bad news for me, it's good news for you. It means I know what steps to take to avoid trouble, and I'm sharing those steps with you. This is another instance when an ounce of prevention is definitely worth a pound of cure. But how do you decipher the mass of information and apply it to your situation? What if they make no sense to you? If you answered yes to these questions, don't worry. I'll tell you why.

Where to Get the Right Answers and How to Make Sure the Answers Don't Change

When it comes to the covenants and restrictions, there's only one place to go for definitive answers: The Architectural Control Committee. This body, or person, has the final say on what you can and can't do in the subdivision. They control the interpretation of the rules. I'm going to give you the proper questions to ask and tell you how to insure you obtain the documentation necessary to keep the answers from changing. If there's any doubt about your particular situation, you must protect yourself.

When you're trying to discover if your project will be allowed, you'll fall into one of two categories. You'll either know you're complying fully with the rules, or you'll be falling into a gray area. The gray area is a bad place to be. For example, let's say you want to install a deck around an aboveground pool you'll be installing. And three of your neighbors, who you know to be in your subdivision, have a similar setup. Plus, you've read the covenants and they specifically state that aboveground pools with surrounding decks are allowed. If this is your situation, you can be assured that your project will be allowed.

If, on the other hand, your neighbors have in ground pools and they're surrounded by patios, and the restrictions don't say specifically that aboveground pools surrounded by decks are acceptable, you'll need to get approval for the project. This is a gray area. In this situation, you'll have to go to the Architectural Control Committee.

If you've followed my directions, you now have a copy of your covenants and restrictions. In the covenants, it will specifically designate who's on the committee and what their responsibilities are. It will also designate a person who is the chairman of the committee. You'll want to start by contacting this individual.

When you contact them, you'll want to have the specifics of your proposed project handy. They may want to know some details that you'll need to have ready for them. They'll want to know what you're proposing, what types of material you'll be using, and where it will be placed on your property. Once you've satisfied their questions, I'm going to have you ask them some questions. In the following bulleted items, I'll discuss these pertinent questions you'll need to ask:

- Is the committee still active? Architectural control committees are set up to be in force for a certain initial time frame. After that time frame has passed, regular meetings are required for them to maintain their control. If the committee has not maintained their regular meeting schedule as outlined in the covenants, they no longer have any control over what you can and can't do in the subdivision. If yours is inactive, read your restrictions carefully to see what rules will govern once the committee ceases to meet, and follow those rules. If, however, they are still active, you'll have to obtain permission from the committee.

- How many members does it take to make up a quorum? This is a fancy way of asking how many members' approval you need to get permission. For example, if the committee has three members, and you need a majority for approval, you'll have to obtain two members' approval. However, you may only need approval of the chairman. Just be sure to get the approval as outlined in the covenants and restrictions. This leads to my last question, which should actually be a demand.

- Can I get approval in writing? Most covenants and restrictions require this, and it is the most ignored rule. We tend to deal on verbal approvals, because it's easier. DO NOT fall into this trap. Most of the time, things proceed without any problems. But, when they don't, you'll come out the loser in the end. Once you have obtained approval, ask for it in writing. Making sure it has the appropriate number of signatures on it. If you are told not to worry about it, nobody ever gets it in writing - WORRY about it. I know I'm suggesting you be particular here, but it's for your own good. If the chairman or other members balk at this request, pull out your copy of the restrictions and show them where it's required. Then, make them comply with the rules like you're trying to do.

I realize that what I've told you to do may seem extreme, but consider it like insurance. When it comes to your home or your health, you can never have too much insurance. The problem with a lack of insurance is you don't realize there's a shortage until it's too late. The same holds true for complying with covenants and restrictions. When you realize you're in trouble, it's too late. And once it's too late, you might as well call your lawyer and open your wallet. You may be seeing a lot of the first and watch your hard earned dollars flying quickly out of the second.

> When it comes to the covenants and restrictions, there's only one place to go for definitive answers: The Architectural Control Committee. This body, or person, has the final say on what you can and can't do in the subdivision.

WHY DO OTHER PEOPLE AND BUSINESSES HAVE A RIGHT TO MY PROPERTY?

Believe it or not, there are certain parts of your property that other people have more of a right to than you do. These areas are commonly called easements. An easement is a portion of your land that is dedicated for a certain use by others. You may not even be able to use the designated area of the easement, although you are required to maintain it in most instances. Let's look at some examples of easements and what they mean to you and your project:

- Utility easements. These easements are granted for over-head and/or underground utilities that run over or under your property. The uses include, but are not limited to, electric lines, gas lines, cable, and telephone lines. You've probably seen an underground warning sign against digging sometime in your life. This sign designates an underground high pressure gas line. The gas line comes with a large easement that runs through the properties that lie over it. What does this mean to the owners of the property? It means that they can put nothing permanent within the confines of the easement. This includes trees, fencing, buildings, decks, patios, porches, and swimming pools. The only allowed use of this area is a grassed yard. But what if I want to fence my yard, you may ask. You can do this. But, if the power company needs access to the easement through your fence, they have the right to gain access however they need to. This includes tearing down your fence. And they're not required to repair it either. But I still want to fence in that area of my yard, what can I do? You ask again. Simply allow them access by means of a gate at either end of your property that allows them to enter and leave the easement at both ends of your property. Then, only in rare circumstances will they need to alter your fence to gain access or to work in the easement. I suggest you install at least a 10' wide gate on both ends of the easement. This will allow them access with any vehicle that can legally travel down the highway without special permits.

- Access to adjoining properties. Easements are often granted through one property to gain access to an adjoining property. You may have a shared driveway or an easement for a future road that would allow development of the property around you. These easements are granted either to keep someone from being landlocked thus cutting them off from their own property, or in the name of "progress", allowing access to future developments. The big issue here can be setbacks. As discussed in Chapter 3, setbacks are the distance you must maintain between lot lines and your residence and attachments to your residence. The setbacks will come into play when you have an easement through your property for a future road. In this instance, an unimproved area of your land may be considered a roadway. This may be undeveloped, but there on paper, roadway or access will determine what is considered to be your front yard and also will determine the setbacks for your home. Check the plat of your property to insure you don't build in, or too close to, any easements that exist on your property.

It may seem unfair to you that other people can tell you what you can and can't do on portions of your property, but think of it this way. Your power goes out and the only way it can be turned back on is if the power company has access to your neighbor's property. You'll be glad they have an easement to gain access and make the repairs they need to get your power back on. It's a necessary evil in this day and age of public utilities. So to protect yourself, check the plat of your property carefully for easements and insure you stay out of their boundaries with your new project.

> There are certain parts of your property that other people have more of a right to than you do. These areas are commonly called easements. An easement is a portion of your land that is dedicated for a certain use by others.

If you don't have a copy of the plat for your property, and you don't know how to obtain one, I'll assume you have not read Chapter 3 of this book. The process is clearly defined there. If you have not read it, and you need a copy of your plat, flip back to it and begin reading. Then you'll have the knowledge needed to obtain a copy and design your project accordingly to avoid trouble.

CAN HISTORY ALTER MY FUTURE?

I want to touch briefly on Historic Districts. If your home is less than fifty years old, this will not apply to you. However, if you live in an older home in an older neighborhood, you'll want to check to see if you live in a Historic District. I've found that many homeowners who reside in such districts have no clue that such districts exist, let alone what they can mean to them and their project. If you fall into the category of not knowing, don't feel bad. Many, many people are in the same situation.

If your home is more than fifty years old, you'll want to check with your local government to determine if your property lies within the boundaries of a Historic District. If it does, you'll need to uncover the process required to get approval for your proposed project. The commission that controls the district will have to approve the plans for the work you are proposing.

The commission will want to insure your project does not interfere with the historic significance of your property. They will be able to dictate many things that you will have to comply with. Here is a short list of some items they may prevent you from using on your home:

- Vinyl siding
- Vinyl replacement windows
- Turned spindles
- Bare treated lumber
- Vinyl fencing
- Aluminum soffit and fascia

This list represents only a few items that may be controlled by the district's commission. For information on how to find out who to contact at your local government, refer to Chapter 3. This chapter explains how to determine what district you lie

FIGURE 4-2
A sign such as this will designate the boundaries of Historic Districts. If you're in doubt of whether you reside in one, or not, contact your local government and erase any doubt before beginning your project.

in and where to begin looking for the proper authorities to contact to obtain the information you need.

SUMMARY

The following list of bulleted items will recap the primary points of the chapter:

- Determine the subdivision in which your property lies.
- Obtain a copy of the covenants and restrictions for the subdivision.

- Decipher if your proposed project is allowed.
- When needed, get permission from the Architectural Control Committee.
- Get this permission in writing!
- Check for easements on your property.
- Design your project to maintain proper distance from these easements.
- Check to insure you do not reside in a Historic District.
- If you do, obtain permission from the Historic Commission before proceeding.

5

Choosing a Design: Preparation of Working Plans and Specifications

I n this chapter we'll discuss how to choose the design that's right for you and how to get that design down on paper so your project will turn out like you've planned. Many choices have to be made before you're through. These include what type of structure/space best suits your needs and your budget. To determine what's right for you, we'll examine several factors then customize your project to fit your specific needs and desires. We'll discuss how you plan to use your outdoor space and what future uses and/or additions you're planning. By looking at all aspects, present and future, of your situation you'll get an outdoor space that's beautiful and useful for years to come.

Another thing you'll have to determine will be the extent and quality of the plans you'll need to proceed. Depending on your location, this can vary from a hand-drawn picture to a full set of architect-drawn blueprints. Either way, you'll need something to ensure your project is a success. After all, a picture is worth a thousand words. And in construction it's no different. Later, in this chapter, we'll discuss the steps you'll need to take to avoid the countless problems I've seen arise between contractor and homeowner because this simple step was overlooked. The contractor had one thing in his mind and the homeowner had another. They both were sure they knew what the other one had in their minds, but neither one was correct. Avoiding this common problem is simple; it just takes a little effort. After you take the steps outlined in this chapter, you should feel confident that your project will proceed to your envisioned conclusion.

WHERE DO YOU START?

Sometimes the hardest part of any task is simply getting started. You want to get moving so you can get what you want, but you don't know where to begin. It's easy to become overwhelmed with the breadth and depth of items that need to be covered. By taking things in order, you can get started and head in the right direction. Let's start at the beginning.

A Basic Idea

First, you need a basic idea of what you want. Outdoor living spaces come in many shapes and sizes. They also have many basic features which will need to be considered. By considering them all, you can wisely pick which one is right for you. We'll look at how you'll use the new area. What are your intended uses? Will it be used during the entire day, or only at certain times of the day? Will you need shade from the sun? Will you need protection from the rain? Do you have small children and/or animals that have specific needs to be considered?

Get a basic picture in your mind of how you intend to use the area. This picture will help you narrow your search for the perfect structure/space. Consider the following points before you move on to look at the individual types of spaces available. The better your understanding of how you plan to use the space, the better equipped you'll be to design it for your enjoyment.

Before moving on, get a piece of paper and a pencil so you can write down your answers to the following questions. Your answers will help you define the space for your specific needs. The way you'll use your new space will become clearer in your mind with each new answer you write down. Having a clear picture of how you'll use the space is imperative to the process of choosing just the right space for you.

- **What will be the space's primary use?** Do you intend to mainly use it entertaining company, or is it primarily for family use? Is it primarily for the children to use during the day? Is it primarily a gathering spot at night? Will it have to house a barbecue grill, toys, gardening equipment, supplies, or anything else? What outdoor furniture do you think you need? Do you need additional space for the items you plan to store on/in it?

- **Who will be using the space?** List the people you expect to use the space. Now rank the people with a 1, 2, or 3. Give each person who will use the space very often a 3, each person who will use the space occasionally a 2 and those that will seldom use the space a 1. By adding up the numbers, you'll quickly get a feel for who the space should be designed for. Don't sacrifice the needs of many people with a 3 for one or two who have a 1. For example let's say you have three immediate family members who will use the space primarily for family barbecues, they all rank 3, and your father-in-law, who ranks a 1, and you have to choose between his needs and yours due to budget issues. Well, I'd hate to be the one to tell your father- in-law, but his needs need to be considered AFTER the three immediate family members' needs. This exercise will help you put your priorities in black and white with a numerical value so you can make wise design decisions.

- **How many people will use the space?** Add up the people you gave numbers to in the last section; how many people are there on your list? Will all these people be using your new space at once? Do they all need their own space in your new outdoor living area? Do you only host them when the weather's nice and the kids are in the yard playing, or do you need cover and protection from the sun/weather for everyone on the list? Consider what people you'll have at your house at once. Do you host large family gatherings? Or do you only have a couple friends over at a time? The number of people you host at one time will determine if you can utilize a small and intimate space, or if you need a large area that can accommodate many people at once.

- **What other area of your house/yard do people need access to when using your outdoor space?** How will they gain this access? Does the space have to be built directly off the rear door of the house? Do you need to add a door to have access to your planned space? Do you want your family/guests to enter where the door is currently located? Or would it be better to relocate it?

Now that you've asked and answered all of the questions, do you have a better idea of how you'll be using the new outdoor space? You should be getting a much clearer image of how you'll use the space by reviewing your answers. Try and visualize in your mind how they indicate you'll be utilizing the space. These images will help you select the style of outdoor space that's right for you.

What Types of Spaces Should I Be Considering?

Now let's look at some particular types of outdoor living spaces. I'll lay out some pros and cons of each type. Compare each space to your list of answers to the questions from the last section. How well does each type of space match your planned uses?

To help you visualize, let's look at an example. Let's say you need a space primarily for you, your spouse, and your son

FIGURE 5-1
Decks are very popular backyard additions. Would a deck fill your outdoor living needs?

and daughter to utilize during the day. Try and imagine your daughter and son playing with their toys on each different types of space. What will you be doing while they're playing? What concerns would you have with each type of space? What advantages does each space hold for your particular situation? Look at each space with your particular needs in mind. I'm going to list three popular spaces for you to consider.

Decks are very popular additions. They can be found in backyards from coast to coast. Decks have many great benefits, including:

- Decks can be built to the height of your existing exits.

- Decks can be built in hard to reach locations where concrete trucks can't travel.

- Deck design and style are almost limitless.

FIGURE 5-2
Patios make practical and durable outdoor living space. Can you
see a patio in your yard?

- Decks can be built from many different materials.

- Decks can be built around existing landscape features.

- Decks can be built over rolling and sloping grounds.

- Decks make great DIY projects because of their straight-forward construction.

Patios are a nice alternative to decks. Some people
wouldn't consider another option. Before making a decision,
consider the following:

- Patios are usually built directly on the ground and usu-ally require steps to enter or exit the house.

- Patios don't need railings to protect children from falls because they're constructed directly on the ground.

- Patios can be constructed from many different materials including concrete, patio block, and paving stones.

- Concrete patios can be colored and/or stamped with decorative patterns.

- Concrete patios can be installed very quickly.

Screened porches shield you from rain, sun, and insects. You can be outdoors, but with the comforts of indoor living. Consider the following before deciding on a screened porch.

- Screened porches are more expensive than decks and patios.

- Screened porches live more comfortably than decks and patios because they shield you from the rain, sun, and insects.

- If not designed properly, a screened porch can look more like an afterthought than an integral part of your home.

FIGURE 5-3
Stamped and colored concrete makes an attractive patio.

- Screened porches often require tearing into your house roof to tie in the new porch roof.

- Electricity can easily be added to screened porches for ceiling fans, lights, and other modern conveniences.

Compare the advantages and disadvantages of each type of outdoor space. Then choose the one that's right for your lifestyle and needs. While this short list isn't all-inclusive, it covers the three most popular applications. At this point if you're still unsure, or are considering more than one option, don't panic. Simply move on to the next steps. You'll gain more knowledge and some cost comparisons to help you further narrow your choices.

CHOOSING BETWEEN THE BASIC TYPES

Let's look at some information so you can narrow your search through the process of elimination. There are many things that will affect your choice. Finances, underground utilities, overhead utilities, size, and landscape features are but a few. Consider the area where you want your outdoor living space. Are there overhead, or underground, utilities that will restrict your choice? Are there trees, rocks, or other landscape features that will restrict your choice?

Consider your budget. Do you have financial restraints that will limit your choice? Have you arranged for financing? Can you eliminate some cost by doing some of the project yourself? Will you be happier with a smaller version of what you really want, or a larger version of the cheaper alternative? For example, your budget allows for a 10' x 10' screened porch which you really want or a 16' x 20' patio which fits your needs better, but isn't your first choice.

Consider the area where you want your outdoor living space. There are many things that will affect your choice. Finances, underground utilities, overhead utilities, size, and landscape features are but a few.

Inspiration

We all need inspiration. When designing your perfect backyard living space, there are many great sources of inspiration. Search magazines, books, and the Internet. You'll find many illustrations showing all sorts of backyard areas. When you see something that catches your eye, try and picture how you and your family would utilize the space you've seen. Will it fit your needs? If not, can you modify it so it will?

The biggest trap here is falling in love with the perfect space, but failing to realize the cost. Many magazines feature great spaces, but many of them come at great costs. Be sure not to lose your realism while you browse. Restrict your search to spaces that will fit your budget, or you'll wind up with a broken heart when you can't afford what you've picked out.

By now you should have a clear picture in your head of how you're going to use your new space. And you should have a fair idea of which types of space will work for you. I'm going to point you in the direction of some additional information to help you narrow your search. Check all of the following sources and glean as much information as you can from each source.

- **Your local library.** Your local library will have oodles of books about construction. It's a great resource for beginning ideas. I say beginning ideas because when it comes to design, the books at the library are typically way out of date. But it's still a great place to start the process of elimination.

- **Friends and relatives with outdoor spaces like you're considering.** Visit and chat with the people in your life who have spaces like you're considering. If possible, spend some time in their space doing what you plan to do with yours. And don't limit yourself to your primary choice. If you have access to a deck, a patio, and a screened porch, spend time on all of them. There's no better way to get a feel for a particular space than to spend time in one.

- **Suppliers, the DIY superstores and the specialty ones.** You can find/get help with prices and styles of many types of different spaces at your local lumber yard or DIY store. They'll have displays of different types of materials. They'll also have books that show many pictures of types and styles of outdoor spaces. Shop around and gather as much information as you can at these stores. Then, visit specialty suppliers such as glass suppliers and concrete suppliers that specialize in only one type of product used in outdoor structures. Use your phone book and your circle of friends and family to get ideas and contact information for different suppliers to check with.

- **Potential contractors.** Potential contractors will be another source for great information. They can answer specific questions and give you rough ideas of cost for each type of project to help you narrow your search. Don't be shy about contacting them for this information. If they want your business, they'll be helpful. This also gives you a first insight into how they conduct themselves and their business.

> The biggest trap here is falling in love with the perfect space, but failing to realize the cost.

After considering these sources, I hope you've been able to narrow down the search for your perfect space to the one that will best fit your needs and budget. You've been able to consider the pros and cons of different types of spaces, as well as some hints at initial pricing differences. You've obtained material pricing from suppliers and some overall costing from some contractors. With this information and all the previously discussed information from the question and answer sessions, you should be able to make an informed decision on your outdoor space.

WORKING PLANS - WHAT THEY ARE AND HOW TO GET THEM

Many of you may be asking what are plans and why do you need them for a simple outdoor project. Let's talk about what they are now, and I'll cover why you need them later.

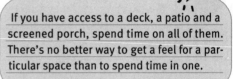

If you have access to a deck, a patio and a screened porch, spend time on all of them. There's no better way to get a feel for a particular space than to spend time in one.

Plans are drawings, or blueprints, that show what you're going to build. They can be elaborate, or very simple. They can be generated on a CAD (Computer Assisted Design) system, drawn to scale or drawn freehand. See Figure 5-4 for an example of simple scale drawn plans.

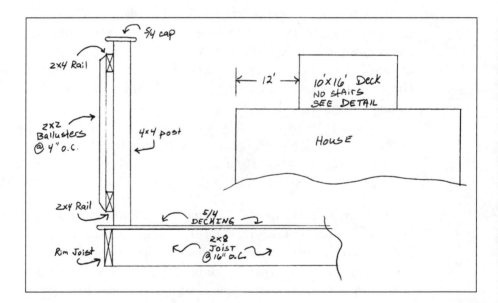

FIGURE 5-4
Working plans can be simple or elaborate. These simple plans were drawn with a pencil and a scale ruler.

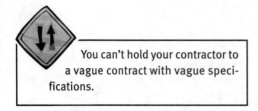

You can't hold your contractor to a vague contract with vague specifications.

There are several factors to be considered when deciding what type of plans you need. The type and scope of plans are as varied as the projects we complete. Everyone's situation will be different. To insure you get what you need, read the next section carefully. I'll cover what steps you should take to determine what's right for you and your situation.

We'll begin by uncovering what, if anything, your local building and zoning department is going to require. If they require detailed plans, your needs really won't come into play. You'll cover your needs by satisfying theirs. On the other hand, if they require little or nothing, you'll have to determine what you'll need to cover your specific needs.

The primary need for plans is for clarification. When you draw a picture, there can be no misunderstanding what the finished product should look like. And if the plans are detailed enough, they will prescribe many more specifics that just layout. Plans can detail fasteners and framing requirements among other things.

What can't be prescribed by working plans will be outlined in the specifications. We'll discuss specifications in the next section of this chapter. For now, let's determine what your needs/wants are as you develop your plans:

- **Local requirements.** To start, let's determine what your local authorities are going to require. To do this, you need to know what boundaries your property lies in, and therefore what building and zoning department's jurisdiction you fall under. If you don't know the answer to this, refer to Chapter 3 to learn how to determine this information. Once you know whose jurisdiction you fall under, look in the local phone book and find the number for your local building and zoning department. Call them and ask what plans they require for your specific project. For many locations, like mine, no drawings or plans are required for residential construction. But, in many other areas of the country, you may need to submit architectural drawings of your project. Whatever the case may be, you'll need to obtain this information from the building and zoning department, and then satisfy their requirements.

- **Your needs.** This section is for those people who were not required to hand in detailed plans to their building and zoning department. I suggest your plans show as many details as they can. The goal is to eliminate any variables that may arise during construction. Items such as hand/guardrail details, footing details, elevations, and stair details should be included. A detailed cross section is also a good idea to show the inner workings of your proposed project. In short, the more detail the better. I recommend you leave nothing to chance.

- **Clarify, clarify, clarify.** The primary goal of plans is to eliminate gray areas, questions, and misinterpretation. Clarify all details in the plans. If you've called out an elaborate cornice detail on your screen room and you're sure that you and your contractor are on the same page, put a detail in the plans. Then there will be NO QUESTION about how it's to be done. I've seen and been involved in countless disagreements where both parties were sure the other party knew exactly what they wanted. A detailed drawing will eliminate all confusion. The plan is the place for drawings and schematics. If you've picked specific materials, call them out in the specifications which will be discussed in the next section.

- **Fancy is not necessary.** Unless required by your local building and zoning department, fancy and professionally prepared plans are not always necessary. Keep your focus on practicality, not beauty. Hand-sketched pictures are often all that's necessary for simple projects. Don't be afraid to sit down and sketch a picture of a detail to insure everyone understands what's expected of them. See Figure 5-5 for an example of a hand-drawn rail detail for a deck. It's simple, practical, and free. But, it serves its purpose well.

> If the plans are detailed enough, they will prescribe many more specifics that just layout. Plans can detail fasteners and framing requirements among other things.

When deciding what you need for plans and specifications, focus on function, not fashion. It's all about eliminating confusion. Unless specified by your building official, it's up to you how elaborate your plans need to be. I'm a firm believer in simple solutions. You really shouldn't need an architect to draw elaborate plans for a screen room. A cross section with a couple of detailed drawings should do the trick. Detailed specifications, which will be discussed in the next section of this chapter, can go a long way to eliminate confusion and save arguments in the future. But when it comes to the way something should look like when it's done, a picture can't be beat.

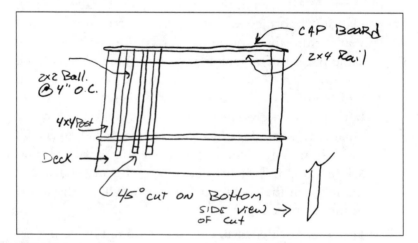

FIGURE 5-5
A simple drawing like this one will eliminate any doubts about what your finished product is supposed to look like.

SPECIFICATIONS - EXACTING, PRECISE, NO QUESTIONS

Do I really need to call out specifics? My contractor is very knowledgeable, shouldn't I trust his judgment? Won't the code official check to make sure everything's OK? These are all excuses for not going through the trouble of calling out specifics or specifications. Believe me, specifics are good. I've never heard of a dispute between parties where everyone's saying that things were over-specified. Disputes and arguments come from confusion and misunderstanding, not from well-explained details.

One thing that has characterized my career in the field of residential construction is that each year I put more specifics in everything. I put more specifics into my conversations, my work orders, my contracts, and my directions. When possible, I'll call out specific items. When I've chosen a specific item, I'll insure the item is listed in the specifics of the contract.

If you've had someone draw up your plans, they should provide you with a list of specifications. If you've purchased packaged plans from your local lumber yard, they will come with a list of specifications. If you've done your own drawings, you'll have to come up with your own list of specifications. If you don't have a background in construction, you'll need help configuring this list.

To clarify, I'm not talking about a material list that lists every piece of lumber, screw, nail, etc. that's going to be used. Specifications should call out for individual items to be used in areas specific to your project, such as structural details and special materials to be used. Check the following list for items you should include on your list of specifics. And keep in mind this list is not all inclusive. You may want to specify items on your project I haven't covered. If this is your case,

> One thing that has characterized my career in the field of residential construction is that each year I put more specifics in everything. I put more specifics into my conversations, my work orders, my contracts, and my directions.

don't hesitate to include them on your list. You can not over-specify. You have a much greater chance of under-specifying. So, if you have any doubt at all, put the item on your list.

- **Structural fasteners.** Many engineers and architects will call out for specific fasteners to be used at structural bearing points. This is can be helpful on large projects. However, for most residential outdoor projects, it may be overkill. Rather than call out for specific fasteners, I would simply point out where special fasteners are required and that all work should be done to your local residential building code and/or the manufacturer's directions. If you have no local code, call out the latest edition of The International Residential Code™. At the time of writing, the latest edition is 2003. If you have a fastener preference, be sure and call it out. For example, if you want the type of screw that won't mushroom the composite decking you're using, then call it out specifically by manufacturer, coating, length, etc.

- **Type and grade of lumber.** Call out minimum grade and type of lumber to be used. For example, you're having a deck built with premium #1 grade, brown treated lumber. Call this out in your specifications. The more detail here the better. Check with your local lumber yard, the one your contractor deals with if you're using a contractor, and have them give you all the specifics for the lumber you're using. If you're using a modern manmade product like Trex®, call it out by specifics.

- **Products you've picked.** This can include siding, roofing, lights, faucets, trim, doors, carpet, tile, sinks, etc. Many stores use a seven digit SKU# to identify their individual products. I use their SKU# in my specifications. This leaves no margin for error and I can list an item with a number rather than listing many details such as manufacturer, finish, size, style and color. I go to the store with the customer before I sign contracts. I show them what material I've estimated, and the alternatives. They then choose what they want. I write down the SKU# and include it on the list of specifications that attaches to the contract. Then, when I've installed an item, there's no question that it's what the contract called for. When not calling out an item by a number, be sure to include the color and style you've chosen.

- **Concrete thickness, strength, and reinforcement.** If you don't know what I'm talking about, don't panic. Your contractor should supply you with this information. You want it included in your specifications so he can't bid one thing and provide another. It's too easy to forget what you talked about before you signed the contract, if it's not in the contract. Get this information, check it with a knowledgeable third party (such as a concrete supplier) to insure it meets standards, and then make sure the work that's done is what's called out in your specifications.

- **Allowances.** When it's not possible to call out a specific item, I'll put in an allowance so no one is surprised when it comes time to handle the left-out specific. For example, when light fixtures must be chosen after the work begins, an allowance in the contract eliminates any doubt as to what amount will be spent when it comes time to buy the item. The homeowner may choose any light fixture they want, as long as it's within the dollar amount of the stated allowance. Let's say you're building a screen room and it will have two exterior light fixtures and an interior ceiling fan and light combo. Unless you have these picked out before you sign a contract with the builder, you can't put in specific fixtures. The contract specifications should reflect an allowance, or dollar amount, and what it's for. It could state: Fixture allowance of $200 for ceiling fan, ceiling fan light, and two (2) exterior lights. The allowance allows the homeowner to pick any fixtures they want as long as they don't exceed the allowed amount.

- **Finishes.** Include all finish textures and paint finishes. If your concrete patio is to be broom-finished, state it. If you want high gloss paint on your trim, state it. Call out colors. Call out drywall, cabinet, door, and trim finishes. For example, if you've specified a wood ceiling clad in WP-4 cedar and finished with two coats of burled marble color, satin finish stain made by Minwax, call it out.

- **Mechanical specifications.** On a simple outdoor project this should remain simple. Let's say you're building a screened porch. An example of the electric specification could be: Install three 110v electrical outlets (one centered on each new wall), one ceiling fan (centered in the room) with light combo controlled by four switches (two to the left of the door to the house and two to the right of the door to the yard), and two exterior lights controlled by two switches (one by the door to the house and one by the door to the yard mounted with ceiling fan/light switches). A description like this one, and a simple drawing on your plans, should leave no question as to what you're getting or where they'll be placed. Items such as heating registers and ducts, plumbing fixtures and placement, phone outlets, and cable outlets should be called out here.

> When light fixtures must be chosen after the work begins, an allowance in the contract eliminates any doubt as to what amount will be spent when it comes time to buy the item.

Remember, the whole purpose of specifications is to clarify. Include any detail you can think of, even if it seems trivial or irrelevant at the time. You can't over-specify. Call out as much detail as you can. And always attach your plans and specifications to your contract. You can't hold your contractor to a vague contract with vague specifications. Detail is the key to a smooth running project.

SUMMARY

Whether you're keeping it simple, or going elaborate, working plans and specifications should paint a clear picture of what you want done. The intention is to have them so detailed you could hand them to someone you've never spoken with and they should be able to build exactly what you want without having to ask a single question. If you've accomplished this, you've done well and your project should run smoothly - at least as far as what's being built and what it's being built with. Check the following recap list to see if your design, plans, and specifications are complete.

> Rather than call out for specific fasteners, I would simply point out where special fasteners are required and that all work should be done to your local residential building code and/or the manufacturer's directions. If you have no local code, call out the latest edition of The International Residential Code.™

> I use the supplier's SKU# in my specifications. This leaves no margin for error and I can list an item with a number rather than many details such as manufacturer, finish, size, style, and color.

- Design to fit your needs, not to look good or to fit the needs of others.
- Design your space for the people who will use it the most.
- Have you looked at how your new space will work with the existing house and yard? Does everything fit and flow?
- Do your plans fit the requirements of the local building and zoning department?
- Have you included everything on your specification list?
- If you gave someone your plans and specifications without saying a word, could they build what you want exactly, without asking any questions?

6

Selecting Suitable Sites for Each Type of Construction

L et's talk about where you're planning to put your new deck, patio, or porch. I say planning because you may change your mind after reading this chapter. I'm going to discuss, in detail, issues that you need to consider when you're deciding where to place your new outdoor living area. I'll talk about elevation, access, underground issues, and several other factors that must be considered when placing your new space.

The last thing you want is to get halfway, or all of the way, through construction only to learn you should have considered _____. The blank can be filled with many things. I'll try and eliminate as many "blanks" as I can for you in this chapter. The only thing better would be if I could personally come to each of your sites and review your plans. For obvious reasons, this isn't going to happen. So, I'll point out the issues I always consider when deciding where to place a new outdoor living area. Read this chapter carefully, plan accordingly, and have fun with your project.

SPECIFIC DETAILS TO CONSIDER

The time to begin enjoying your new space is now. As you are pondering the points I make in this chapter, use your imagination and picture your family and friends all gathered on the new space doing what you enjoy doing when you get together. This will accomplish two things. First, it will help you take some of the stress out of design and construction, and second, it will go a long way in helping you to place the new space exactly where it should be to fit your needs.

Use your imagination and picture your family and friends all gathered on the new space doing what you enjoy doing when you get together.

You can't design the perfect outdoor space without considering how you're going to use it, and you can't pick the right space for your situation without considering where it's to go, how it's going to fit against the house, and how you'll get to it.

You have to have the proper access to your space not only for use, but first and foremost, for construction. For this reason, it's good to think through all aspects of your project before you begin. Do you have access for workers and materials?

Think about a typical gathering you'll have in/on your new space. Imagine who'll be there and what they'll be doing. Watch their actions in your mind. Picture where they're going as they move around, going about their business. Where do they enter and exit the outdoor space the most? Are they going in and out of the house for food and beverages? Or are they moving between the yard and the new space? Keep this information on your mind as you go through this chapter, it will help you in determining where the best place for your new space is.

I'm going to cover specifics for decks, patios and porches separately. Then, later in the chapter, I'll cover items that will affect them all. There are design features unique to each type of structure that will need to be discussed for that particular type of space, and other features of your yard, under your yard and over your yard that could affect all three types. But let's start out covering each specific space individually.

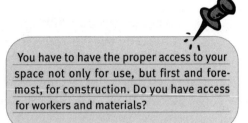

You have to have the proper access to your space not only for use, but first and foremost, for construction. Do you have access for workers and materials?

The Deck

The deck is one of the most, if not the most popular type of outdoor living area utilized in the United States today, and for good reason. It's inexpensive, easy to construct, and flexible. By flexible, I don't mean you can bend them, I mean they will adapt to many situations. This adaptability is one of the issues we'll discuss in this section. More to the point, how several features will, or will not, adapt to your particular situation.

I'm going to discuss elevation, rails, and building around features in your yard. Each topic will be discussed as it pertains to decks only. I want to pinpoint features and considerations so you can choose the best place for your new deck. If you've designed the perfect deck for you and your family, you don't want to regret where you place it in your yard. You also don't want to find out too late that one of your most important reasons for choosing a deck has now been made ineffective because of your placement. Read the following and consider how the points covered apply to your specific situation.

> If you've designed the perfect deck for you and your family, you don't want to regret where you place it in your yard.

The Highs and Lows - Elevation

Does your yard slope? If so, how will that affect your deck? If it doesn't slope much at all, or if it slopes towards the house, do you even have room for a deck? Before you can answer these questions you have to know how much slope you have in the area you plan on placing the deck. To determine this, I'm going to give you two simple options. First option: You can take a board, a level, a tape measure, and a friend to the location you want to place the deck. Have your friend hold the board under the threshold of the door you're building in front of, or where you want the height of the deck to be, and you take the other end of the board away from the house. Place the level on the board until the bubble is centered between the lines in the glass of the level. Now take the tape measure and measure from the top of the board to the ground. This will tell you how much working room you'll have while building your deck. However, if your end of the board is sitting on the ground and is not level, meaning it needs to go further down to reach level, you will have to move dirt to build your new deck. And, you'll have to buy wood rated for underground if the frame will rest in the ground. If this is your case, you may want to consider a patio, rather than a deck. Moving dirt and buying lumber treated to the higher retention required for underground applications is expensive. A patio may prove to be a better option for you. Or, you can figure out a new place to put your deck and avoid the grade problem. Is there another place in the yard that's more suitable for a deck? Can you still achieve your desired uses in the new location? Check the other possible locations with the board and level to see if they'll work better for you.

The 30" Rule

Another thing to consider is that you'll need guardrails on any portion of the deck that is more than 30 inches above grade. This means you'll only have access to the deck where you build a staircase or have an interior door. If you envisioned the kids running on and off the deck in all directions, but you have to have guardrails, this will change your vision. An alternative to consider would be to build the deck in sections and lower each section of the deck to correspond to the lowering grade. You'll also want to consider stairs and their size if your deck will be many feet above the yard below. Stairs will become expensive and take up lots of yard space in this instance. Consider where you'll have to put the stairs. You'll need an area 3' wide by whatever length your stairs need to meet code. This means you need 1.39' of length for every foot of height. For example, your new deck will be 6' above grade. This means your stair case will be 3' wide x 8.34' long. The 8.34' was calculated by multi-plying 6' (the height) by 1.39 (the multiplier). You can con-vert the fraction to 16ths of an inch if you'd like. The idea is to give you the rough size of your stairs so you can place your deck accordingly.

> Another thing to consider is that you'll need guardrails on any por-tion of the deck that is more than 30 inches above grade. This means you'll only have access to the deck where you build a staircase or have an interior door.

Can I Build Around That?

This question is commonly asked because of an existing yard feature that the homeowner really doesn't want to lose. But the features must be moved or accommodated if the deck will be built where they want it. Usually, before really knowing what's possible, they resolve the issue by conceding the fight. They say something like, if I put my deck where I want it, I'll have to cut down that tree. Or I'll have to move my sidewalk. Or whatever the obstacle at hand it is. This simply is not true. Decks can be built in endless shapes and sizes. It's true, most of them are rec-tangular or square, but they don't have to be. They can, and are, built to varying shapes and around varying obstacles everyday. You simply need to measure your desire for what you want against what the cost will be. Elaborate patterns and odd shapes come at a price. It's not as economical to build around some-thing as it is to build a big rectangle. While material cost may not rise, labor costs can go through the roof. But don't give up without at least considering exactly what you want. Consult with your contractor and ask him to compare the price of what you want against the norm, or what seems more practical. If you

If you will have to move dirt to build your new deck, you'll have to buy wood rated for underground if the frame will rest in the ground. If this is your case, you may want to consider a patio, rather than a deck. Moving dirt and buying lumber treated to the higher retention required for underground applications is expensive.

can't build around your feature, consider moving your deck to a new location.

Patios

Patios are my personal favorite if the house sits close to the ground. Patios allow for unlimited access to your surroundings. You can enter or exit them at any point. When I have multiple guests, people can come and go simultaneously in many different locations without impeding each other's progress. Without rails to inhibit the edges, when a patio gets full, a person can sit in a chair that's half on and half off of the patio and still feel like they're on the patio. This way it can effectively "grow" to fill the immediate need.

Patios can also be constructed of many materials and can be an easy DIY project. But, an improperly placed patio can cause problems. Selecting the right location and making sure it will work for you is imperative. Let's look at some particulars as they pertain to patios. Pay close attention to all the details. By doing so, you can place your new patio in the optimum location for you and your family.

- **Elevation.** Elevation is the most critical element for a patio. Sloping grade is not patio-friendly without a lot of work. If the grade slopes away from your house, you wind up with a massive blob of concrete, sand, and/or stones at the edge of your patio. If the grade slopes towards your house, you wind up having to dig a hole and install a retaining wall to hold back the potential mudslide. I'm not saying that these situations are always unacceptable, but you need to be aware of the requirements for installing a patio on sloping grade. Check your elevation as outlined in the previous section on decks. If your grade elevation changes less than

12", installing a patio should not be difficult. However, if it slopes more than that, you'll have to do some extra work during installation. Check with your potential contractors, your local library, and your local lumber yard for ideas on how to handle the slope in grade. An alternative to digging holes or having a massive edge to your patio is to install your patio in multiple levels following grade. Installing your patio this way will section off your patio and make it less useful than a single level, but may be a desired end result to the added work and expense of the alternatives.

- **Stairs.** Unlike the stairs on a deck, stairs to your patio are usually constructed on the patio. This means they take up space on your patio. Instead of building to the height of your door as is done with a deck, patios are constructed on grade. Then steps are built from your threshold height to the level of the patio. If this distance is small, under 15 1/2", a single step will suffice. One step takes up minimal room. If the distance will be greater than this, multiple steps will be required which will take up considerable space on your patio. Another consideration for stairs is the requirement of a 3' x 3' landing if a door swings out over the patio or steps. Figure this space in your design if you have an out-swing door.

- **Access for the big truck.** When deciding where to put your patio, don't forget if you're pouring concrete, the truck has to be able to get to you. If this is not possible, at a minimum you'll have to be able to get a concrete hand truck to the site. I poured a concrete floor under a sun porch in 1989. The location was in the rear yard. The grade on the side of the house descended 8' in 30' of travel. I can tell you that a cubic yard of cement in a hand truck will take you for a ride. If you must deliver your cement by hand, or have it done, I urge you to be careful and consider your situation. Not only will this cost you more money, it can be dangerous if the truck is too heavy to control on your steep grade. Talk to your supplier or contractor for any guidelines they have for this situation.

- **Unique designs and designing around existing features.** Patios can be built in almost any shape and around most existing features. The patio on the rear of my house has a sweeping edge. The front edge is similar in shape to the center of a yin and yang symbol, or the edge of a teardrop. Framing the sweep took a little time, but is not an impossible task by any means. If you're a person who thinks outside of the typical square that everything is built to, use your imagination and let your creative juices flow when designing. You can build your patio in places that a deck would not be practical. You can sweep it around trees, bushes, flowers, and landscaping with minimal added effort. Consider working around obstacles and don't rule out a desired location.

Patios allow for unlimited access to your surroundings. You can enter or exit them at any point.

Patios are flexible, and provide unlimited access at the perimeter. For these reasons I prefer them as an open outdoor living space. Consider the previous points when deciding where to place your new patio, remembering to consider designing around existing obstacles before moving from your preferred location. Cement can be hand delivered with a hand truck when access by a full-sized concrete truck is impossible. Consider your grade and the weight of the hand truck when filled for you and your worker's safety.

Porches

Screened or unscreened, a covered porch is a nice addition to any home. You get the joy and beauty of the outdoors, but you're still protected from the sun, rain, and bugs if your porch is screened. Finding the right location for a covered porch is more difficult than finding a location for a deck or patio. You can use a wooden, stone, or concrete floor for your porch. So you not only have to consider all the points for your floor, you must look up and consider the requirements for installing a new roof. Much of this planning and deciding on location will vary with what type of roof you're going to install. Flat roofs take up much less space and require less room than pitched roofs. However, a well-designed pitched roof that matches the home's existing roof will make your added porch look like an integral part of the home, not some slapped on as an afterthought.

I'll discuss particular points to pay attention to when deciding the best place to install your new porch. I won't re-cover the issues discussed for decks and patios, you'll want to consider those issues as well, but there's no reason to write them twice. Simply read the previous section that deals with the type of floor you plan to install.

The points I'm going to discuss are particular to porches. Read them carefully and consider your desired site to see if it will work for your application.

> Flat roofs take up much less space and require less room than pitched roofs. However, a well designed pitched roof that matches the home's existing roof will make your added porch look like an integral part of the home, not some slapped on as an afterthought.

- **Look up.** When placing your porch, you must look up. Consideration has to be given to where the new porch roof will mount and attach to the existing structure. You must consider if the new roof will interfere with existing features of the home. Are there windows that will be covered? Are there utility lines that need to be moved? These lines include electric, cable, phone, and condensing lines for central air conditioners. You must consider how you're going to tie the roof into the existing house. How will the roof attach to your siding? Will you be able to make a watertight connection where you have it currently placed? Can you make modifications so the new roof can connect without moving it? Are these modifications possible and, more importantly, will they fit within your budget? All of these questions must be answered before you begin construction on the site you've chosen. If you have questions and concerns, be sure and cover them with your contractor and/or the building inspector. If you're a DIY'er, consult with someone who has the needed knowledge and experience to answer your questions.

- **Integral part or slapped-on addition?** If you place your new porch carefully and design it properly, it will look as if it has always been on the house. However, if you don't pay attention to detail or misplace the addition, it will look just like what it is - an added-on section of the house. Your goal should be to make the addition appear as if it has always been there. This means placing it where it flows with the existing floor plan. How do you plan to access the porch? Will the porch interfere with other existing areas of the house and/or yard? Can you move the addition to better appear as an original portion of the house? How will you tie the porch foundation and the house foundation together? Can you tie the roof lines in to match the existing roof? Are you going to create a drainage problem with the current placement of the porch? Will the new roof line flow aesthetically with the existing roof lines? Can you tie new gutters in with the existing ones? All aspects of the new porch - siding, windows, roofing, soffit, fascia, gutters, foundation, etc. - will have to flow with the existing counterparts of the house to make it seem like it's always been there.

- **Yard features.** Wrapping a roof around a tree is much harder than wrapping a poured concrete patio around one. Existing features should be given more careful consideration when placing a covered porch than when placing a deck or patio. If you have tree that your father planted and you don't want to remove it, you have to consider how its future growth will affect your new covered porch. Will the tree eventually grow into the roof? Will you have to trim it back severely to keep it off your new structure? If you have an existing feature that you don't want to remove, can you build the roof over or around it? If the new porch is to be used only in the summer, can you leave a section of the roof out to accommodate the feature? This option won't leave the room watertight, but will provide cover from most of the elements. This may be an option if you refuse to move the porch and/or the existing feature. If you do build around a tree or other vegetation, don't forget to consider the future growth of the tree or vegetation. A small tree can grow into a large one over several years. If you want your porch to be useful and practical for many, many years, you must consider how it will be in the future. This includes how your vegetation, children, and neighborhood will change over time as well. These future considerations are discussed in more detail later in the chapter.

Consider all the aspects pointed out when placing your new outdoor living space to avoid regrets. After all, what good will your new space be if you misplace it? Even if it's use-

> When placing your porch, you must look up. Consideration has to be given to where the new porch roof will mount and attach to the existing structure. You must consider if the new roof will interfere with existing features of the home.

able, you'll always have that nagging feeling that you should have placed it somewhere else. You can avoid regret by giving careful thought and examination to where you're placing your new space. Try and picture the new structure. Picture not only how it will be placed, but also the features around it and how you're to use it. A carefully thought-out plan and course of action will save you not only time and money; it will insure you get the most out of your new space.

GENERAL OBSTACLES TO AVOID

Some seen and unseen features of your yard and house must be considered despite the type of structure you'll be building. Universal threats to the proper choice of placement of your structure exist in your yard, on your house, and under the ground. The key to successful placement includes being aware of these threats and either avoiding them altogether or having a plan to deal with them if they get in the way. The best strategy is to avoid them altogether if possible. While this is easy in concept, it becomes very hard or even impossible in practice sometimes. The idea is to be aware of them before making the final decision on placement and considering the possible ramifications at the onset of your project. Sometimes being aware of the potential for a problem, and sharing that information with your contractor, is all that's needed to avoid it. On the other hand, some things are just better left alone. I'll walk you through the primary things that must be considered to avoid an unknown factor, and the potential for the problems it can cause once it becomes "known".

The key to successful placement includes being aware of these threats and either avoiding them altogether or having a plan to deal with them if they get in the way. The best strategy is to avoid them altogether if possible.

The "Invisible Problem"

Many potential problems lie under the earth, or simply are not tangible issues, so they can not be seen. So the question then becomes: If I can't see it, is it really a problem? The answer is yes, and no. If a tree falls in the woods, does it make a sound? Yes it does, but you're not there to hear it so what do you care? Some people take this attitude with unseen potential for problems on their jobsites. Sometimes they get away with it, and sometimes they don't. For example, when I was having my pond dug, I was aware of a water line that ran in the vicinity of the pond site. The line had been run without permission and without an easement, so the authority in charge of the line was to move it before we began digging. So, I notified them several times before the excavator arrived to begin work. The authority had the option to take care of the unseen potential for problems, but they failed to do so. The end result was a broken water main and free filling of part of my pond thanks to the authority. This time the tree fell and everyone heard it! Don't let yourself get into a similar situation. Read this section carefully and avoid the potential problems by identifying the unforeseen *before* everyone "hears and sees" them.

- **Plumbing lines.** These lines include water service lines, septic lines, and sewer lines. Take the time to identify where your plumbing lines enter and leave your house. If your home has a crawlspace or basement, this is a simple matter of locating the line and seeing where it exits the foundation. If, however, your house is built on a slab, it will be more difficult to locate these lines. The key is to know where they leave the house, and where they go after that. If they travel in the vicinity of where your new outdoor structure is to be erected, you must determine if they will be an issue during construction. Will the line be in the way of footings? Is there an access or cleanout that needs to be moved so you can put your new area where you want it? If the line fails in the future, will the new area prohibit its maintenance or replacement?

- **Electric service lines.** Not only can these lines be a nuisance, they can be very dangerous. I once had an excavator cut a line and shut down power to an entire city block. Luckily no one was hurt, but the mayor wasn't real happy that he was without power for several hours waiting for the repair crew to fix the damage. If you have a line entering where you'll be digging, notify your contractor and his excavator so they can take the proper precautions to avoid getting anyone hurt.

- **Yard flow.** Mark off where your new outdoor living space will be. Use stakes and string to simulate the size and height of the new space. For example, you're building a new deck that will be 12' x 16' and will sit at the height of the threshold of your sliding glass doors. Get eight stakes and ample string. Set four stakes at the corners of where you're planning on placing the new deck. Now set the remaining stakes at the corners of your stair case that will lead to the yard (if you plan on

FIGURE 6.1
If your electric lines enter your service from underground, like the ones in this illustration, be conscious of where the service wires are when digging for your new outdoor living space.

having one). Run the string around each set of four stakes at the height of the proposed section of your new structure. Now, in your mind, run through your usual activities taking the new deck into consideration. Visualize yourself mowing the yard, playing fetch with Fido, baseball with your son, and having that long-awaited barbecue with your friends and family. How does the new structure work where it is? Can it be moved or altered and fit in better? Do you need to alter the height or move the staircase so it fits in with your activities?

> If plumbing lines travel in the vicinity of where your new outdoor structure is to be erected, you must determine if they will be an issue during construction.

The Visible Problem

Many possible deterrents to outdoor living space placement are visible. To find them you just have to look in places you may not have thought of. They may be on your roof, hanging in the air, on the ground, and some may only be visible at certain times of day and/or certain times of year. I'm going to list the primary ones you should be on the lookout for, but don't exclude any others that come to mind. As I've said before, a well thought-out design and plan of action will save you from many potential headaches and pitfalls down the road. If you can visualize the final product and how you plan to use it, you will avoid many potential problems by "seeing" your new structure and its uses. If you have a hard time visualizing your new structure and its uses in your mind's eye, use props. You can use a card table and chairs to represent patio furniture and you can use a handheld umbrella to simulate a larger free standing model. Sit where your new structure will be. Now read this section and take a look around you. Relate your application to the potential problems I'm about to list.

- **Electric, phone and cable service wires.** In the previous section, I talked about underground electric service. In this section, let's discuss overhead service. Look up from where you're sitting. What do you see? Are there electric wires overhead? What about phone or cable wires? Are they within reach of your new outdoor living space? If they are, check with your local codes to see what the required clearances are. For safety's sake, if your kids can possibly reach them, move either the wires or your new space. OK, let's say they're out of reach, but still overhead. Do birds land and sit on them over the planned site of your new space? Will you alter or change anything that will encourage them to? If you've ever seen an area under a wire that's popular with the birds, you'll know why this can be an issue.

- **Plumbing and heating vents.** If you're putting a cover over your new outdoor living space, or if you think it's a possibility in the future, you have to make sure you don't cover up or eliminate the necessary clearance around plumbing and heating vents. These vents are usually PVC pipe or galvanized pipe and extend through the roof of your home. They may not be covered up. Also try to design or place the new structure such that an existing vent does not wind up in the valley where the new roof ties into the existing roof. Protrusions through the roof should be kept away from valleys to avoid leaks and damming of ice and snow.

  > If you're putting a cover over your new outdoor living space, you have to make sure you don't cover up or eliminate the necessary clearance around plumbing and heating vents. These vents are usually PVC pipe or galvanized pipe and extend through the roof of your home.

- **Permanent obstacles.** This can include items such as sheds, fences and well caps. Keep in mind when placing your structure that you not only have to be able

FIGURE 6.2
An overhead wire where birds accumulate usually has a mass of
bird dung under it. Place your outdoor structure away from or
move existing lines to avoid this unhealthy hazard.

to maintain the yard between these items and your new
outdoor living space, but you may have to maintain the
items themselves. If you have to get in to replace your
well pump, will you have access to get equipment and
workers to the well for maintenance? If you have to
replace a fence, gate or other item, can it be done
without tearing up your new outdoor living space? See
Figure 6.3 for an example of bad placement.

- **Vegetation.** To avoid space issues in the future, you
  have to plan for how big a bush or tree will be, not how
  big it is now. When placing your structure, take into
  consideration how big the surrounding trees and bushes
  will get. That cute little blue spruce beside your new
  deck will grow into a behemoth over the next decade or
  two. You'll have to place your new outdoor living space

FIGURE 6-3
This patio was placed too close to this well. If the well casing ever needs maintenance or replacement, the patio may have to be dug up to gain the necessary access.

away from the tree, or plan on trimming the tree to an unnatural shape and size to accommodate the space.

Placement of your new structure is important. Consider all of these items carefully to properly place yours. One of the keys to proper placement is to visualize not only how you intend to use the deck in the near future, but also for years to come. The next section of this chapter covers future considerations and how to plan accordingly for them.

PLANNING FOR THE FUTURE

The only thing that stays the same is change. Your life and how you live it is no exception. Your family may grow or shrink.

You may make new friends who love to spend time outdoors, or not. Countless factors will determine how much you use your new outdoor space in the future. What we want to do in this section is examine the ones that can be controlled so you can place your new outdoor living space optimally for future use and enjoyment.

While there are no crystal balls to consult, you can predict future uses by looking closely at several factors that you know will come to pass. For example, you know that your daughters, aged 15 and 17, will be going off to college soon and your need for space will go from large to small. By examining issues like this, you can place your space properly.

I'm going to cover several areas to consider that will affect how you use your space in the future. Consider each one carefully when deciding where your new outdoor living space should be built. The idea is to optimize current needs and uses with your future needs and uses. This may sound difficult to some of you, but it's not. Looking to the future may simply help you to plan better. I recommend you weigh the importance of both current and future needs and design according to what fits your lifestyle and needs the most.

- **Future expansion.** Will you want to expand your outdoor living space in the future? Are your children young and will their needs grow along with them? Are you on a limited budget now, but think you'll want to add more space in the future as money allows? Do you have older parents who may come to live with you in the future? If any of these scenarios fits your situation, place your new outdoor space so you can expand it in the future.

- **Future reduction in use.** Are your children about to go to college and reduce the amount of time you spend in your new outdoor space? Will their leaving change the way you intend on using your yard? Are your children young enough that their growth will change the best place for your new space? Should you place the new space in a corner of the yard to allow a larger central play area for them as they grow? Should your new outdoor space be located in an area that will make it more accessible as you age?

- **Pets, plants, and pools.** Do you plan to get pets in the future? How will a pet affect the use of your yard and the placement of your outdoor space? Do you plan to add trees or a garden? Is a pool in your future? If you're planning any of these listed additions, take them into consideration when placing your outdoor space.

By looking to the future changes in your family and the way you plan to use your new space, you can effectively place it in the perfect spot for your future needs. Give careful consideration to all the issues listed.

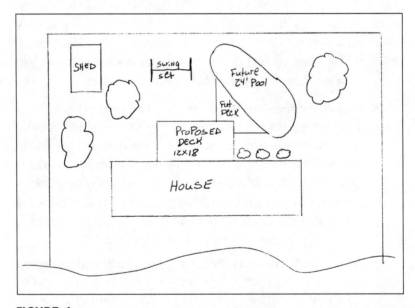

FIGURE 6-4
This picture shows you how you can "map" out your future plans to consider when deciding where to place your new outdoor living area today.

The key is to sit down and think through the way your life will change over the next two years. Then think about five years from now. Now go to ten years down the road. When you think of these future times and your needs, consider what will be important to you at that time, and plan accordingly.

SUMMARY

Proper placement of your new outdoor living space will help insure you get the optimum use and satisfaction. Review this list of points from the chapter. Consider each point carefully. If you're unsure of what I'm calling for, go back and reread this chapter until you understand the point. If you consider all of the listed points, you'll be able to place your new outdoor living space in the best possible location for you and your family.

- Consider how the elevation of your lot will affect your new space.
- What yard features, present and future, will affect your new space?
- Will your new space tie into the existing house and look like an integral part of it, or a stuck-on afterthought?
- Beware of underground and overhead utilities.
- Allow for future use, expansion and/or maintenance of your new space and its surrounding features.

7

Hiring a General Contractor

Selecting the right contractor is like culling crops. You must disregard the weak, the camouflaged, and the unreliable. The first step in weeding out bad contractors is to go to the telephone. Telephones are the arteries of strong remodeling and home- improvement firms. Communication is critical to a satisfying job. When you begin your search for contractors, you start with the telephone. Your phone will see a lot of use before and during the remodeling or improvement venture. There will be questions and concerns about the project. When they arise, you will need to be able to contact your contractor. The phone can tell you much about a contractor before you ever talk to the business owner.

Answering machines are disliked by almost everyone. When you take the time to call a company, you expect to get information right away, not after the beep. Recorded messages are offensive to many people. Others think it is rude to have a business phone answered electronically. If a machine answers your initial call to a contractor, what will your opinion be? Answering machines are used for many different reasons and do not necessarily indicate a bad or disreputable contractor. Maybe the contractor spends much of his or her time supervising or working on jobs. These are two qualities to look for in a good contractor. When the general is on the job, fewer problems occur.

A positive aspect of answering machines is that they keep overhead costs down. Receptionists and secretaries increase overhead significantly and may be unnecessary for small firms. As a customer you pay for increased overhead, which is passed on through higher prices. The contractor with an answering machine may be less expensive.

Some contractors use answering machines to screen calls. This is not a desirable trait. Contractors who screen their calls usually have dissatisfied customers or hounding creditors. There is a way to distinguish between the two purposes of an answering machine. Call early in the morning and again around 6:30 P.M. See if the contractor answers the phone. The contractor using a machine to keep costs low will probably be coordinating work at these times and should answer your call personally. The machine will answer the phone 24 hours a day, acting as a buffer for the undesirable contractor.

Regardless of their purpose, answering machines eliminate your ability to talk with the contractor immediately. Even if the contractor checks for messages regularly, you will not be able to reach the contractor right away. This can be a pivotal problem if something serious goes wrong on your job. All you can do is leave a recorded message, with no way of knowing when your call will be returned. This could be reason enough to disqualify the contractor from your consideration.

When you begin the search for contractors, keep a log. Enter the contractor's name, phone number, the date, and the time you called. When the contractor returns your call, note the time and date in the log. This may sound excessive or silly, but it can tell you a lot about a potential contractor.

You might be surprised by how many contractors will never return your call. It continually amazes me how contractors can

PHONE LOG

Date	Company Name	Contact Person	Remarks

remain in business without returning phone calls. A successful contracting company depends on new business, and the refusal to return phone calls is business suicide. Some contractors will return the call but only after two or three days. The phone log helps you spot these red flags.

Contractors should return your initial call within a few hours. If the contractor is working in the field, it may be evening before your call is reciprocated.

If it takes this long to speak with the contractor, there is a problem. Slow response to a request for new work means no response to calls about work done poorly. Contractors should return your initial call within a few hours. If the contractor is working in the field, it may be evening before your call is reciprocated. A good contractor will tend to present clients first and then potential customers. Although your message may receive lower priority, you should not have to wait days for a return call.

Phone response is an important element in choosing any contractor. If a contractor uses a receptionist or personal answering service, he or she can be reached quickly. The answering service should be capable of paging the contractor or calling him on the job site. Many contractors have a mobile phone or truck radio and will check in with the service periodically.

In today's competitive market, most successful contractors utilize cellular technology. Ask the answering service when your message will be conveyed to the contractor and how long it will be before you can expect a call. Write the information in the log, then wait and see if the time estimate was accurate. You shouldn't base a remodeling or home-improvement decision on the empty promise of a rapid response.

There should also be a way for you the reach the contractor immediately in a crisis situation. An answering service can promptly relay your call for help; an answering machine cannot. A cell phone is even better.

Two hours' turnaround time is acceptable when you are not an existing customer. Once your job is started, your calls should be returned within an hour or less. There should also be a way for you the reach the contractor immediately in a crisis situation. An answering service can promptly relay your call for help; an answering machine cannot. A cell phone is even better. Overhead costs for the contractor remains low with an answering service, and the phones can be tended 24-hours a day. For the small contractor this is the sensible solution to the phone challenge. For the consumer it is an acceptable arrangement, combining fast phone responses with lower contract prices.

Contractors with administrative personnel and offices offer consumers a sense of security. The customer can go to an office and speak with the contractor or his office staff. Unless the contractor is doing a high volume of business, you will pay more for these conveniences. This secure, professional appearance can also be misleading. Offices and administrative assistants don't make good contractors.

Finding the right contractor requires attention to detail and a well-conceived plan. A phone log is only the beginning, as it allows you to eliminate some contractors right away. If they don't perform well in your phone test, they won't perform well on your job. Delete contractors who don't promptly return your call; they obviously don't want or need your job. If they don't care enough to return your calls, forget them. You are looking for a good contractor with a desire to do your job. Ask them questions and record their answers on paper to keep in a file. Keep a list of the subcontractors with whom you may work.

Do not be lulled into a false sense of security by outward appearances. It is possible that the office rent hasn't been paid for in months or the administrative staff is from a temporary service. The office furniture and equipment could be on a monthly lease. You can't judge contractors on appearance alone.

Your Company Name
Your Company Address
Your Company Phone and Fax Numbers

SUBCONTRACTOR QUESTIONNAIRE

Company name: _____

Physical company address: _____

Company mailing address: _____

Company phone number: _____

After-hours phone number: _____

Company president/owner: _____

President/owner address: _____

President/owner phone number: _____

How long has company been in business? _____

Name of insurance company: _____

Insurance company phone number: _____

Does company have liability insurance? _____

Amount of liability insurance coverage: _____

Does company have worker's comp. insurance? _____

Type of work company is licensed to do: _____

List business or other license numbers: _____

Where are licenses held? _____

If applicable, are all workers licensed? _____

Are there any lawsuits pending against the company? _____

Has the company ever been sued? _____

Does the company use subcontractors? _____

Is the company bonded? _____

With whom is the company bonded? _____

Has the company had complaints filed against it? _____

Are there any judgments against the company? _____

SUBCONTRACTOR LIST

Service	Vendor	Phone	Date

The right contractor will understand your needs and strive to meet them. There are good contractors available, but finding them can be a challenge. Like any good result in life, locating the right contractor takes time. You will have to look hard to pinpoint exceptional contractors, and inducing them to do your job may take some creative maneuvering. These high-demand contractors have plenty of work. Don't despair; there are ways to attract the best contractors.

> Delete contractors who don't promptly return your call, as they obviously don't want or need your job. If they don't care enough to return your calls, forget them.

Where should you start your contractor quest? The Yellow Pages are a logical answer. Here you will find contractors who have been in business for awhile. It takes time to get into the book, and the advertising rates are steep. If you really want to do your homework, check the phone company for back issues of the Yellow Pages. You can chronicle a contractor's business history by noting the size and style of the ad over a period of time. The general contractors listed cover every aspect of construction and remodeling. Many of the ads will list the contractor's specialties. You must sift through the list to find suitable contractors for your job.

Advertisements in the classified section of your paper are another good resource for names. These contractors are probably either hungry or starting in business. Cross-check to see if the contractor is also listed in the phone book and Yellow Pages. Here is a quick tip on telephone advertising. If the contractor advertises in the paper as "John Doe Building," he should also be listed as "John Doe Building" in the phone book. If you find a listing in the white pages for "Mr. John Doe" and no Yellow Page listing, you can assume he operates from home without a business phone number. If you don't find "John Doe Building" in the line listings, he is probably a rookie or part-timer.

This isn't always bad. John Doe may have years of field experience with other contractors. This background can override the lack of business experience, and you might get your best deal from John Doe. If Mr. Doe tells you he has ten employees and has been in business for fifteen years, be cautious. The phone company is not in the habit of allowing people to operate a business from their home without paying additional fees. Official businesses are customarily given a free line listing in the phone book. A little research can go a long way in testing the validity of a contractor.

Another effective way to find contractors is by doing some undercover work around your neighborhood. Look for jobs in progress on other houses. When you see a contractor's sign or truck, write down the name and phone number. Jot down the address of the house where the work is being done. These jobs can be future references to check for potential contractors.

> Jobs under construction often yield easy access and allow you to see the contractor's work. If you like what you see, call the contractor and ask if he or she is interested in bidding your job.

Explain that your house is close to the one the contractor is working on; ask to walk through the job in progress with the contractor. Finished jobs are much more difficult to gain access to because homeowners don't appreciate a parade of people going through their recently renovated house. During the remodeling process, homeowners expect a lot of traffic. Take advantage of your timing, and go see the work while you can. If you get the opportunity, ask the homeowners if they are satisfied with the contractor and the work.

Do you know anyone who recently had renovation work done? Friends and acquaintances are a reliable resource, because you get the names of tradespeople who have done satisfactory work for people you know personally. Do not take this information as the absolute solution to your contractor search. Before running out and signing a contract, ask yourself a few questions. Was the work done for your friends similar to the work you want done? If they had their bathroom remodeled, it doesn't automatically qualify the contractor to build your dormer addition. A contractor capable of building exquisite decks isn't always the best candidate for extensive kitchen remodeling.

Networking among reputable contractors increases the chances of finding a good contractor for your job.

Make sure the contractor is qualified to complete the work you want done. If not, consider contacting the contractor and asking for references of other tradespeople in your specific area. Good contractors do not associate with unprofessional, amateurs who might tarnish their reputations. Networking among reputable contractors increases the chances of finding a good contractor for your job. Mentioning that you were referred by a fellow contractor or satisfied customer also carries a lot of weight.

The first step in finding the right contractor is establishing your needs. Make an outline of the type of work you want done. Do you plan to build a garage? A competent contractor in bath and kitchen remodeling may not be the best choice to construct your garage. The bath contractor works with existing interior conditions, as opposed to footings, site work, or rafters. Check out your contractors carefully and compare their qualifications to your specifications.

Many remodelers are specialists in their field. Remodeling has become increasingly complex and can be compared to medical services. Would you go to a pediatrician for advice on a heart condition? A dormer addition requires a specialist, experienced in cutting open a roof and the many structural changes involved. The knowledge required for work of this magnitude is different from the experience needed to finish a basement. The company that did a great job on your neighbor's basement could prove to be a disaster for your dormer addition. Whenever possible, you want to compare apples to apples and to differentiate the knowledge and skill needed for the job at hand.

There is almost no comparison between building a dormer and finishing a basement. Basement work doesn't usually

OUTLINE OF WORK TO BE DONE

GARAGE CONSTRUCTION

Choose style of garage desired.

Draw a rough draft of garage or obtain a pre-drawn plan.

Make or obtain a list of required materials.

Select materials to be used.

Price materials.

Make list of contractors needed or a list of general contractors.

Contact contractors.

Obtain labor quotes.

Evaluate budget needs and ability to afford the garage.

Make financing arrangements.

Make final decision on plan to be built.

Choose contractors and check references.

Meet with attorney to draw-up contracts and other documents.

Make commitments to suppliers and contractors.

Schedule work.

Start work.

Inspect work.

Obtain copies of code enforcement inspections.

Make required payments and have lien waivers signed.

Inspect completed job.

Make punch-list, if necessary.

Make absolute final inspection and approval.

Make final payments, except for retainages.

Make retainage payments.

(continues)

OUTLINE OF WORK TO BE DONE (continued

CATEGORIES OF WORK TO BE DONE

Survey	Framing	Painting
Blueprints	Windows	Electrical work
Permits	Doors	Insulation
Site work	Sheathing	Drywall
Footing	Roofing	Electric door
Foundation	Siding	openers
Floor preparation	Trim work	Landscaping
Floor		

---

require any structural expertise. A contractor doesn't have to contend with inclement weather or rafter cuts. Finishing a basement has its own challenges with support columns and altering existing conditions. Proper care to control moisture is another skill necessary in finishing a basement. With a dormer contractors have to know how to deal with rain, wind, and snow. Most of the work is new construction, and existing conditions only play a small role. The contractors who execute these jobs can be as different as the two types of work performed. A comparison will show both types of contractors are professionals in their field.

There may be a few contractors capable of doing both types of work well, but this is the exception rather than the rule. Finding a well-rounded, fully experienced contractor is rare. The majority of contractors specialize in closely defined areas of remodeling, which are determined by several factors. Some contractors concentrate on the jobs offering the highest profit, and others specialize in work they enjoy. You must determine a potential contractor's weaknesses and strengths. Usually the work a contractor does most often is the work he or she does the best.

The fields of specialization can cover any aspect of remodeling and improvements. Some examples include:

- Garages can be a specialty.

- Sunrooms are a common specialty.

- Dormers can be a specialty.

- Additions offer the opportunity for specialization.

- Kitchens are a natural specialty.

- Bathrooms are one of the most popular rooms in a home to remodel.

Some companies stress their special talents through advertising. The bulk of newspaper ads consist of newer businesses. Many haven't been established long enough to get in the Yellow Pages. Newspaper ads and fliers are easy sources of effective advertising for young businesses.

> Contractors just starting out can be an inexpensive alternative to get your job done. With the right precautions, new businesses can result in exceptional values.

New businesses need your work and will try very hard to win your job. Your negotiating power is stronger with these contractors. While they are new in business, they may be extremely good at what they do. They may have years of experience working for another company, and experience is what you are looking for. It doesn't matter where they learned to do the job as long as they do it right. The contractor who sits behind a desk for five years could have less experience than the tradesperson just starting a

> There is some risk to a new company, since it is more likely to fail. This will result in trouble when a warranty problem arises. You could get well into the remodeling process, only to have the company close its doors. Getting another contractor to come in to finish someone else's work isn't easy, and it will be expensive. To reduce this problem, stay in control. Be prepared for the worst and never let the contractors have more money than has been earned.

business. Your interest is in their remodeling experience, not their business degree.

Rules of the Road

- Do not be afraid to use a new company; the savings often offset the risks.
- Maintain control.
- Don't give the contractor a large cash deposit.
- Put everything in writing.
- Inspect all work closely before advancing any money.
- Insist on lien waivers when any money is paid.
- Ask for original certificates of insurance before any work is started; these should be provided to you without delay from the insurance company.
- Ask for three credit references.
- Obtain several job references.
- Follow up on the references and ask to see actual examples of the contractor's work. It's easy to give friends and relatives as job references, so check them out personally.
- Request evidence of the contractor's state and local license numbers.
- Ask for the contractor's address; this will make a bad apple squirm.
- Validate and investigate all the information to protect yourself against the unforeseen.

These basic rules should be used with any contractor. A company in business for ten years can be out of business in a day. The longer a company has been in business, the more time they've had to get into financial trouble. Businesses that grow too fast sink even faster. From the outside, a company can look extremely successful even when it is in deep trouble.

Shiny new trucks, fancy offices, and large management staffs are impressive but expensive. A company with these expenses must compensate for its overhead with volume or higher prices. Any company with extensive overhead is a potential bankruptcy case. And this can be bad for you.

A contractor may have been successful for the last several years and still get in trouble fast. A growing business, with heavy overhead can be derailed by a slow economy. If the company's

> You can be hurt by either an established company or a new one. You have to protect yourself at all times.

volume of business declines, it can't afford its overhead. Items such as a fleet of trucks and expensive offices quickly consume any reserve capital. When this happens, a once successful company fails. Don't be fooled by an impressive exterior appearance. Keep your guard up, and make all contractors play by the rules.

If you find a contractor from newspaper or Yellow Pages ads, be selective. Call enough contractors to get a fair assessment of the talent available. Evaluate each contractor. Ask questions, get everything in writing, and don't assume anything. It is important to establish a position of control from the beginning. Reputable contractors will respect you for

> Experienced contractors will be happy to answer your questions, and they will put their answers in writing. This process will eliminate much of the competition, and reputable contractors appreciate an informed consumer.

your knowledgeable business practices. If you know enough to ask the right questions, the quality contractor will get your job. They don't have to worry about the fast-talking, hard-selling, low bidder. When you are ready to schedule your subcontractors, make a written record of the schedule.

Good contractors constantly fight the price-war battle with questionable contractors. They have to survive without using the

SUBCONTRACTOR SCHEDULE

Type of Service	Vendor Name	Phone Number	Date Scheduled

Notes/Changes:

slick tactics of less honorable companies. Regardless of the game, playing by the rules is the hardest way to win. In the remodeling arena there are a lot of people looking to win at the customer's expense. The best contractors are in business for the long haul, and your satisfaction will mean more business down the road. They know you will call again for future work or refer them to your friends. Word-of-mouth advertising is the best a contractor can have. It is inexpensive and produces a consistent flow of good work.

Contractors living on the dark side will not have these concerns. They are looking to make a fast buck. They aren't building a business. They're making money. Their objective is to get your money, and they operate on a one-shot basis. In larger cities they survive because of the turnover of residents. In many urban areas a contractor can get to you before his reputation does.

Large cities are a perfect breeding ground for shoddy work. The environment allows renegade contractors to run rampant. They know their present customers aren't likely to affect future business. All these contractors concentrate on getting jobs so they can get the customer's money. Many contractors have refined this approach into an art. They utilize good advertising and trained salespeople to thrive in the city. They know all the ways to stay one step ahead of you. Unfortunately, their methods are legal, and their tactics are well defined.

They prey on uninformed homeowners. With demographic studies they can attack the market of their choice. These are not contractors. They are professional sales forces. When selling to first-time homeowners, they may arrive in a compact car so as not to appear overly successful. The objective is to appear on the same financial level as the consumer.

When working a different neighborhood, the vehicle of choice may be a four-wheel-drive pickup truck. This is the "Good Ole Boy" approach, designed to assure you that the contractor works just as hard as you do for his money. Such salespeople will wear jeans and flannel shirts, with boots and a tape measure. They will take notes on a metal clipboard to give the illusion of a working contractor. Some people respond better to a general contractor who works on the job himself. These camouflaged salespeople prey on a homeowner's weaknesses. They know how to do it and make their living selling jobs. I have seen these people in action. They often sell more jobs than the workers can complete. It's up to the scheduling department to juggle irate homeowners like hot potatoes.

In upper-class neighborhoods, these birds of prey arrive in a luxury car: wearing a three-piece suit and carrying a leather briefcase. Laptop computers and gold pens will be part of their arsenal of sales tools. This is the "Dress For Success" method,

Use common sense, and never allow yourself to be pressured or persuaded into a commitment.

giving the contractor the image of a dynamic, prosperous businessperson. He acknowledges that your time is valuable and points out that his is, too. He suggests that he can squeeze you into his busy schedule if you sign the contract tonight.

Is this the kind of game you want to play? It shouldn't be, unless you are willing to lose. These sales-oriented professionals seldom have any field experience in remodeling. It is likely that they use subcontractors for all the work. Their prices will be inflated to allow a hefty profit for their time; you are probably paying them a commission to sell you the job. Why should you keep them in expensive suits and luxury cars? Cut them out and enjoy the money yourself; you probably know as much about remodeling as they do.

A call to the Better Business Bureau or Contractor Licensing Board can tell you if the contractor has been reported for adverse or illegal business practices.

Calling a contractor you know nothing about is risky. A business card picked up from the community bulletin board could produce a good deal or a remodeling rip-off artist. Advertisements in free newspapers deserve a phone call, but be wary. There are unlimited ways to find good contractors. The tricky part is finding a suitable contractor for the type of work you want done. Not all contractors are created equal. Some are better than others in specialized areas.

Don't sign anything without thinking and without reviewing the documents. Ask about material and work guarantees, and be sure to get them in writing. Requiring the contractor to use your contract will immediately weed through many of the sharks. Remove their fancy clauses and legal rhetoric and you pull their teeth. Swing the pendulum in your favor in every way possible. Read books and research your project before dealing with any contractors. Try to get a referral if at all possible. Do your homework before having work done on your home.

8

Avoiding Underground Obstacles

If you can't see it, it can't hurt you...right? Wrong! It can hurt you, cost you money and time, and, in the worst case scenario, it can kill you. Now, before you get too excited and/or scared, almost all residential construction jobs end up with everyone still alive in the end. However, bad things can and do happen. What we want to accomplish in this chapter is to identify the things you can't see, but should be aware of - mainly utilities.

I'll discuss several factors to consider before allowing anyone to dig on your property. I'll start with why you should be aware of underground utilities. Then I'll move on to share some of my personal experiences and the legal reasons for being informed. The chapter will close with how to get the information you need to be safe and how to actually conduct safe digging on your site. This chapter is going to cover a lot of information. Read it carefully so you can keep everyone safe and save time and money by following the proper procedures during the construction of your outdoor living space.

WHAT ARE UNDERGROUND UTILITIES?

Underground utilities are wires or pipes that are under the ground and can include gas lines, electric lines, cable lines, and phone lines. What many of us don't realize is that they are everywhere around us. (Or better put, everywhere under us.) Depending on how long ago your neighborhood was developed, you could have anywhere from a few to all of your utility lines run underground.

A simple way to check for underground utilities is to take a walk around your house. Look for the places of entry for your gas, electric, phone, and cable lines.

A simple way to check is to take a walk around your house. Look for the places of entry for your gas, electric, phone and cable lines. Do they come up from under the ground to your house, or do they come in overhead? Do some come up and others down? It will be different for many of us. The thing to remember is that even if none of your utilities come in from underground, you still have underground lines on your property. You have the sewer line from your house and possibly public lines elsewhere on your property.

AVOIDING UTILITIES

Now that you know you have underground utilities on your property, let's talk about why you should take the time to be aware of where they are located. For you the homeowner, the easy way out at this point is to think the contractor will take care of all this. I've had some pretty reliable contractors who just didn't bother, and others who simply forgot to do what was necessary. The fact of the matter is that attitudes toward safety and taking the extra, easy step vary widely. I know some contractors who simply refuse to dig without following the rules. On the other hand, I know successful contractors who have found themselves in trouble over and over again, but still refuse to follow the rules. It's hard to discern exactly what attitude your contractor will have until you ask.

So, what do you do? You read the information contained in this chapter and make sure your contractor follows the rules. You may be asking why you should have to have knowledge and take care of things that your contractor

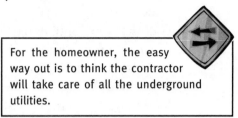

For the homeowner, the easy way out is to think the contractor will take care of all the underground utilities.

should know and be taking care of. The reason is because even the best-intentioned people make mistakes and occasionally overlook things that need to be done. So you have two choices. You can take a little time and insure things are done right or you can trust someone else with all aspects of your project. Since you're reading this book, I trust you're going to do the right thing and ingest the information written here. Then you'll watch over your own project, making sure things are done correctly, every step of the way.

Why Bother Locating Utilities At All?

This question is asked often. The answer, in a nutshell, is to be safe. Now the obstacles to safety are numerous. It's our job however, either as contractors or as homeowners, not to get lazy or in a hurry. You also need to make sure you don't succumb to the obstacles so the jobsite runs safely. Nobody reading this book wants to see someone else get hurt. Or much less, get ourselves into trouble for not following the law.

Sometimes the reasoning for not being safe seems practical - being safe can cost time and money. Time and money are usually in short supply on jobsites. First, things always get delayed, which puts the project behind schedule. Whether due to the weather, a late subcontractor, or a multitude of other reasons, projects always seem to start and/or run behind schedule.

The excavator was supposed to be here last week, but it rained. Or the plumber was supposed to rough in the drains under the slab, but his previous project went over time and he couldn't come until Friday instead of Monday like he said. And, as we all know, time is money.

Another reason for not being safe is simple forgetfulness. How many times have we turned around and remembered something we were supposed to do, but forgot? We're all human; we forget things. Contractors are no different. The excavator shows up and no one has called for the dig locator. Oh well, it's too late now. And we dig anyway. This is unsafe and should be unacceptable. But sometimes, in the name of time and money, we consider it worth the risk. This is the wrong attitude to have. I'm going to list some reasons and give some examples of why it's very important for you to have your underground utilities located before you begin digging on your property.

Why Bother? I've Never Hit Anything Before.

This is one of many attitudes I've seen displayed. Let me list some others that can stop you from taking the time to have your utilities located:

- I don't have time to wait.
- I'll deal with it if I hit something.
- I know where all the lines are already.
- I've done some digging around here before and never hit anything.

I've heard them all, and, much to my chagrin, I've succumbed to too many of them. Sometimes things went OK, and other times things were disastrous. Don't take or make excuses. Do the right thing and have your utilities located.

Examples of Disasters

Let me give you two examples from my experience. In both of these examples, I tried to do the right thing. However, I left the ultimate decision to my excavators on whether to call or not. I **should not** have done this. If you're in doubt as to whether your excavator or contractor has had the undergrounds located, do it yourself. I wish I had.

In the first example, I needed a trench cut for a water line that was to feed a house I was building. My plumber had no equipment, but my neighbor did. My neighbor offered, very nicely, to dig the trench for me. I was grateful. I asked him to call me when he was getting ready to dig and I'd call JULIE (JULIE is our statewide locating service) so the utilities would be marked. He agreed. About three days later, I received a call stating that I had better get out to my jobsite. And I'd better make it quick. I was told the mayor was very upset and people were talking about lawsuits - not to mention a man **could have been killed** on my jobsite!

I was shocked. I went out right away. My neighbor had sent his man out to dig the trench with a backhoe without telling me or having the utilities located. The digger cut the underground power line which shut down the electric service for three city blocks. The mayor just happened to be home and lived in one of the houses that were without power. He was furious, to say the least. The backhoe being used to dig the trench had a quarter-sized hole in the bucket from the electric shock and the driver of the equipment was lucky to be alive. All of this happened because someone got in a hurry and I didn't cover my own jobsite by calling ahead.

In the second example, I was having a pond dug. I was aware of a water line that ran right through the dig site. I called the water company two weeks before we began digging but no one showed up. I called again within a week of digging and no one showed up. I called again the day before the digging was scheduled to start. Again, no one showed up. So, my excavator dug. And guess what? He hit the water line. My pond got a quick fill up for free and everyone down line from the dig site lost water for the better part of a day and then had to boil their water for the next two days after the hole was fixed. All this trouble happened because someone was lazy. I've shared these two examples so you'd know that things can and do go wrong. Sometimes even deadly wrong when the simple step of locating your underground lines is skipped.

It's the Law

If you don't have your underground utilities located before you dig in your yard, you're breaking the law. This means whenever you dig. If you're putting up a bird feeder and you have to dig a hole for it, you're supposed to call. If you're installing a fence and you have to set the posts, you're supposed to call. And if you're digging footings for your new deck, you're supposed to call.

Sometimes, in the name of time and money, we consider cutting corners to be worth the risk. This is the wrong attitude to have.

So, I hope I've given you enough information to stress the importance of having your underground utilities located before you do any digging. It's a simple thing to do. So do yourself, your family and your contractor a favor - call to have your underground utilities located before you dig.

LOCATING UNDERGROUND UTILITIES

If you're like most people, you've never had to deal with the underground utilities on your property. If you haven't, consider yourself lucky. This means you've never had a problem with them that needed your attention. If you've ever talked with someone who has lost electric service, water service, gas service, or sewer service due to a problem with an underground line, they'll quickly let you know what a problem it can be.

But we're not discussing problems, we're discussing improvements. Right now you're concerned with NOT creating problems with your improvements. To do this you'll have to locate every underground utility line on your property. But don't panic, it's not as hard as it sounds.

I've discussed why it's important to locate your utility lines and this section of the book will tell you how to locate them. Once you discover how easy and cheap it is to have them located, you'll wander how anyone would skip this simple step to insure safety on their jobsite.

Locating Underground Utilities

In two words - you don't. Someone will do this for you. All you have to do is call the proper phone number and someone will come out to your jobsite and mark the locations of your underground utility lines. It's that simple.

OK you say, but what's the cost? Well sit down and hold on to your seat, because it's free! It won't cost you a dime! Location is provided to you at no cost as a public service to help keep workers and the public safe from harm. Do we live in a great country or what?!

So the big question remains, how do I locate mine? If you have access to the Internet, type in this link: http://www.rentrain. com/targetrental/underground1.html. The link takes you to a site that lists the dig safe numbers by state. Once there, click on your state and the information will be displayed. Follow the instructions for your state. Most of the time, this is handled by calling a toll free phone number.

If you don't have access to the Net, this toll free number is usually available in your local phone book. If you don't have a phone book or can't find it there, call your local power company or local building and zoning department. They will be happy to provide you with the toll free number to call for service.

When you call, be sure to have the information they require as listed on the website. It's also important to have the site properly identified and marked. In my state, the property must be clearly labeled with an address and the work site (where the digging is to occur) must also be clearly marked. This allows the workers who mark the location of buried cables/lines to easily locate your property and have a clearly defined area of where the work is to be performed.

While on the phone with your dig safe office, they will give you a dig number - write this number down! It is very important that you keep this number on record. If you or one of your contractors has a problem during the course of digging, this number will prove that you followed the proper steps and the law. You can prove you called to have your utilities located and that you followed the time frames set forth by law. Without this number, all you have is your word that you did as you were supposed to.

After you've called your dig safe number, workers will show up and begin marking the location of the underground utilities. There will be several who will visit your location. They will mark their lines or paint an OK on the ground to indicate the lack of lines on your property. This process usually takes up to 48 hours.

When the locators have done their job, your underground utility lines will be marked with paint and/or flags. At this point, and only at this point, is it safe and legal for digging to commence on your property.

Safety Doesn't Stop With Identification

Just because you've identified where the lines are, doesn't mean that everything is perfectly safe. You, or your contractor, still have to exercise some precautions while digging in the vicinity of buried lines. It's not as simple as it seems. To be safe, read the following points carefully.

- **Close, but no cigar.** Your locator came out and marked your buried utilities. That means they're directly under the mark, right? In two words, not necessarily. The locators are allowed a margin of error of up to three feet. This means their mark can be up to three feet off the actual line, and still be within acceptable tolerances.

- **Dig carefully within 3' of the mark?** No. The mark can be wrong by three feet to either side of the underground line. This means you must be careful over an area that covers 6'. See Figure 8-1.

- **So, I should get out a shovel and put away the backhoe?** Absolutely. No power equipment should be used near the marked line. Abandon the easy way and pick up a shovel. A word of caution - shovels, spades, picks and post hole diggers can still puncture underground lines.

- **All underground utilities are at least 3' deep. Wrong!** You should dig carefully, and by hand, from the surface down. For example, I was digging a post hole over a buried gas line. I figured the line was at least 2' deep and I was digging 2' to the left of the mark. I began digging normally with my jobbers. At approximately 12" I felt resistance when I tried to pull the dirt. I sent my jobbers out of the hole. Baffled, I pulled out the tool and began clearing the dirt away from the obstruction with my hand. I figured I had found a tree root in my hole. But, much to my surprise, I found the gas line. It was right between the indents the blades of my jobbers made. If God had not been watching out for me, I would have severed the line in two, putting me and the whole neighborhood at risk! If I had turned the tool even a quarter turn, I would have sliced the line off clean! So, be careful from the ground down. You never know how deep a buried line is, or how close to the mark it is, until you find it.

- **The bottom line is, be careful. Be slow. Be safe while you dig around underground lines.** You can't see them. They're very dangerous and even deadly. Don't play around. Be safe and dig slowly.

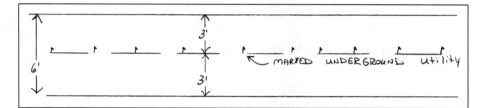

FIGURE 8-1
Buried utility lines can be up to 3' away from the marks locating their location. This means you should dig carefully by hand on 3' of either side of the mark.

The simple, free, and quick process outlined in this chapter can save someone's life, please don't skip it! Don't let anyone talk you into circumventing the law and being unsafe in the name of speed, schedules, or dollars. No amount of money will replace what could possibly be lost.

Following the law is quick and easy and should be your goal before allowing anyone to dig on your property. Go to the website, find your dig safe number, and call. You'll be glad you did.

9

Choosing a Suitable
Type of Foundation

S uitable. What does that mean? Or better put, what does it mean to you on your project? Well, in actuality, it can mean many things. It can mean it fits. It can mean it's what you can afford. It can mean what looks the best in your situation. And it means other things as well.

It can, and will, mean different things to different people. It won't be the same for you as it might be for your neighbor or your best friend. It will vary from person to person and situation by situation. Our goal, in this chapter, is to guide you to the best foundation for you and your outdoor living space. To accomplish this, we'll discuss many topics and ask many questions about your particular situation.

You'll want to write down the points that you think apply to your situation and discuss them with your contractor. It's always good to get his input as well. The idea behind this chapter is to cover the points you need to make an informed decision as to the type of foundation that suits your situation the best. Your contractor will no doubt have some suggestions and preferences for you to consider. This chapter will arm you with the information needed to weigh the options he gives you.

While the choice of foundation style and type may seem simple and obvious to some of you, others will want some direction to make the best possible decision. If you fit into the category of wanting more information before making a decision, this chapter is being written for you. I want to give you some points to consider. Then I'll provide some practical things to add to the considerations, and then finally I'll provide some preferences based on my experience.

After you've finished reading, I hope you have a clear understanding of what type of foundation you want, why you want it, and what you expect it to do for you. For you to arrive at this decision, I'm going to direct you to not only think of today, but to consider many tomorrows as well. If you have the perfect outdoor living space built today, but it fails to meet your needs of tomorrow, what real worth would it have? The space would become much less valuable when it ceases to meet your family's needs. Let's start the foundation selection process by considering some initial points of interest and possible concern.

FOUNDATION CONSIDERATIONS

There are several points you need to think over in your quest for the perfect foundation. I'm going to point out the major areas you should consider and list the reasons you should spend some time pondering them. This list is not all inclusive; every situation is different. If you find you should also be giving consideration to another factor, don't exclude it simply because I haven't listed it. It would take a book in and of itself to cover every issue in every possible situation. And, this chapter can't cover them all!

While reading over the points and considering the implications of each point as it applies to your foundation, keep in mind that the proper choice must meet your immediate **and** your future needs. Every one of our situations will change over time. Give consideration to your future needs and possible changes in your life and use of your outdoor space. In the years to come, you'll be glad you did. Consider these points carefully before deciding on the proper foundation for your outdoor living space:

> Keep in mind that the proper choice of foundation must meet your immediate **and** your future needs.

- **How do I intend to use my outdoor living space, and who will be using it?** Making the proper choice involves knowing how you intend to use the space, and also who will be using it. Picture in your mind the details of your outdoor space. Will you be entertaining large numbers of people? Do any of your possible guests or family have special needs to consider? Do you have special uses in mind to consider? For example, you plan to add a barbecue pit made of stone in the future. This will have to be considered now, when you're designing the space, to allow for the future addition of the pit.

- **Can I use an open foundation, or does it have to be closed?** First, what do I mean by open or closed? An example of an open foundation would be a pier foundation as is commonly used under many decks. A closed foundation is a continuous foundation wall such as a block wall or a poured concrete wall. Second, why does this matter to you? The answers include affordability, usability, and nuisance reasons. For example, if you live in a wooded area and you have an open foundation, it's only a matter of time before you have critters move in to take up residence under your new outdoor living space. On the other hand, if you live in an urban area, building codes may prohibit the use of some types of open foundations.

- **Load.** The sole purpose of your foundation is to support your new outdoor living space. In order for you to choose the proper one, you must know what kind of weight it will be supporting. In most simple cases, your local building codes will outline what is required. However, if you plan on extraordinary uses, you must plan for an extraordinary foundation. The reasons for beefing up your foundation can be many. You could throw large parties where your new outdoor living space will be very crowded and you need to accommodate the increased load, or you could be adding a hot tub or other heavy object to your space at a later date. These extra loads will need to be accounted for in the foundation.

- **Future development.** Will you need to add utilities to your outdoor structure at a later date? Will you be closing in above or below your deck in the future? If so what foundation considerations need to be made now so you're ready for your future updates? Will you be adding a roof in the future? Consider all planned and possible future expansion and their impact on your choice of foundation. It's much easier to design for future expansion from the start than it is to redo an undersized or inadequate foundation in the future.

- **Matching your existing foundation.** Should you consider matching your existing foundation? In a word, sometimes. If you must use a foundation similar to your home due to code or grade issues, by all means match your existing foundation. However, if you don't have to use a continuous foundation, you should give ample thought to using a pier foundation for ease of installation and for budgeting concerns. My only advice here is that if you plan to, or if you think others will plan to, close in your outdoor living space, you should match your existing foundation so the "addition" doesn't look like an addition. Instead, by matching the foundations, it will look as if it

An example of an open foundation would be a pier foundation as is commonly used under many decks. A closed foundation is a continuous foundation wall such as a block wall or a poured concrete wall.

were always there. If the foundations match and careful attention is given to the details, an addition can look like an original part of the home.

By considering the following points, you'll begin to get a feel for which type of foundation will work best in your situation. It may even remove all doubt from your mind and you can skip the rest of the chapter. However, if you're still unsure, or would like some more information, read the rest of this chapter and I will provide all the additional information you need to make a well-informed decision.

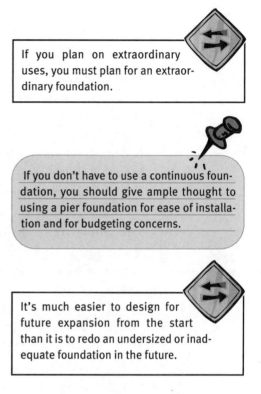

If you plan on extraordinary uses, you must plan for an extraordinary foundation.

If you don't have to use a continuous foundation, you should give ample thought to using a pier foundation for ease of installation and for budgeting concerns.

It's much easier to design for future expansion from the start than it is to redo an undersized or inadequate foundation in the future.

PRACTICAL CONSIDERATIONS

Most of you reading this book have to be practical about what you do. I'm assuming you're not independently wealthy and therefore must consider your choices carefully. The key to being practical is to not lose your head. Many things would be nice, but are far from necessary. Take, for example, a natural stone foundation. A natural stone, or even cast stone, foundation would be an excellent and aesthetic addition to almost any home. However, paying for one is another story. The problem is that what's practical is not always what's best. And the most practical is not always the least expensive.

So, the key here is to try and find the foundation that is the most practical to use, and the most practical on our wallets. This is often easy, but at other times it is not. I'm going to outline some points to consider so you can make an informed decision and choose the best possible foundation for your new outdoor living space:

- **Open or shut?** How much space will there be under your new outdoor living space? Can you utilize this space? If there's enough room for storage, will it be a space that is practically used, or will it just collect junk? If you plan to use this space, should you leave the sides open, or should you close them in with a solid material? If it's usable, is it within your financial budget to close in this area?

- **Too close for comfort?** If your new outdoor living space needs to be close to the ground to match the height of your home, will you have to excavate a hole for the foundation? Is there a more practical type of foundation or structure to use in this instance? If the digging will become extensive, or alter the use and look of your yard, should you consider an alternative structure or foundation?

- **Sloping grade.** Does the grade of your yard slope away from your house? How much does it slope within the length of your new outdoor living space? If the slope is excessive and you're planning a continuous foundation, would it be more practical to use piers? If it slopes sufficiently, can you utilize the space under your new outdoor living area? Can you cantilever the joists over a load-bearing beam to keep the supports closer to the house?

- **Code.** Will your local code allow for pier foundations? What specifically are your options according to the local code? Are there local or regional concerns such as bedrock or soil with very low load-bearing capacity that will limit the options for your foundation? Are there local indigenous materials that meet or exceed your local codes that can be used in your foundation to save you money? Is there a code-accepted alternative foundation you can use to lower your overall costs? For example, an alternative for a screened porch might be an insulated slab foundation in lieu of a crawlspace that matches your existing foundation.

A natural stone, or even cast stone, foundation would be an excellent and aesthetic addition to almost any home. However, paying for one is another story.

At times, it's hard for us to be practical. We want what we want and we don't care about what's practical and what's not. However, in many instances, being practical can not only save you dollars, it can make your new outdoor living space function better as well.

If your new outdoor living space needs to be close to the ground to match the height of your home, you may have to excavate a hole for the foundation.

The previously listed items will hopefully get you thinking about your situation in ways that you hadn't thought of before. The idea is to think through as many possibilities as you can, and choose the one that's best for you and your new space. We all want beautiful

For a screened porch, an insulated slab foundation, in lieu of a crawlspace, that matches your existing foundation could be the answer.

spaces. But, I ask you, what good is a beautiful space if it's not practical? And if your foundation isn't practical, the function of your new outdoor living space won't be practical either.

MY RECOMMENDATIONS

Some of you may still be confused as to what's best for you and your situation. For those of you who are, I'm going to list my preferred foundations for some common applications. You don't have to agree with me, it's alright if you don't. I don't mind.

You may have particular reasoning for using something other than what I prefer. These reasons can include regional differences, contractor preferences (if a contractor does not like installing a particular type of foundation, he'll typically charge more for it to persuade you to use his own preference), or matching considerations. I'm not trying to talk you into using my preferences. I'm merely providing some information for the people who are still undecided at this point:

If a contractor does not like installing a particular type of foundation, he'll typically charge more for it to persuade you to use his own preference.

For decks, I prefer to use deck blocks. However, these blocks are not always allowed by local code.

For a covered porch, I prefer a poured concrete and pier or post foundation. The total load of the porch and the covering must be included when sizing your footings and your supports when using this approach.

- **Decks:** For decks, if it's allowed by the code, I prefer to use deck blocks. However, these blocks are not always allowed by local code. So check before you commit to their use. These blocks allow a deck to be built independently of the house and allow you to start building without any digging and or messing with concrete. You don't have to wait for the footing to set up before you begin to build. Simply set the block down on a level spot and start to build over it.

- **Porches:** For a covered porch, if it has no possibility of being walled in at a later date and is being constructed of wood, I prefer a poured concrete and pier, or post, foundation. The total load of the porch and the covering must be included when sizing your footings and your supports when using this approach. If the porch floor is to be concrete, I prefer a continuous masonry foundation that matches the existing house's foundation. If budget is a concern, a wooden porch on a pier foundation is much more reasonable in price than the concrete porch with a continuous masonry foundation.

> Follow the guidelines for the material used for the floor of the screen room before choosing the foundation.

- **Screen rooms.** This situation calls for following the guidelines for the type of material to be used as the floor of the screen room. If the floor is to be concrete

> If the patio has no chance of being walled in at a later date, no foundation is required.

FIGURE 9-1
A deck block is an easy, quick and inexpensive foundation for a deck. Make sure to check your local building codes to see if they're acceptable in your area.

FIGURE 9-2
A continuous foundation is required under a porch slab. The foundation material under the porch should match the material used in the house foundation.

and insulated, slab would be my preference for a foundation. If the floor will be wood, I prefer footings and piers or posts - don't forget to add in the weight of the walls and roof when calculating the size of foundation required and check with your local codes to see if this application is allowed.

- **Patios.** If the patio has no chance of being walled in at a later date, no foundation is required. The only time you would need to incorporate a footing or foundation is if the patio will eventually be walled in or covered with a roof that will rest on top of it. Otherwise, a simple slab on grade works well in this application.

As I stated before, you may or may not agree with my preferences and that's OK. You have to decide what's right for you and your outdoor living space. Everyone's situation is different and calls for different material and applications. Consider all your options and consult with your contractor, your supplier, and your building official. Then choose the foundation that's best for you.

SUMMARY

The perfect outdoor living space must start with the perfect foundation. If the foundation isn't suitable to your application, the rest of the space won't be suitable either. If you've read this chapter carefully, you should have the information you need to make the proper choice.

For review, read the following bulleted items and consider each one carefully. Consult with your contractor considering all the points from this chapter that are applicable to your situation. After all, contractors must build from the ground up, and the foundation is where it all starts. Choose the proper foundation for you and your outdoor living space to get your project off and running in the right direction:

- Will/can you use the area under your outdoor living space? If so, design your foundation to allow access and coverage to fit your needs.

- Allow for future development in the foundation. If it's at all possible for you or future residents to expand or add to your space, design accordingly. An example would be if you'd add a roof over or screening around your space in the future.

- Does your foundation need to allow for future addition of any utilities such as electrical wires or plumbing pipes?

- Should your foundation match your home's foundation so your new space looks like an integral part of the home instead of an addition to it?

- If the grade around your house slopes to or away from the house, carefully consider how this will affect the appearance and cost of your chosen type of foundation.
- If you can't decide, review my foundations of choice to see if they'll work for you.

10

Sample Pricing to Keep Your Contractor Honest

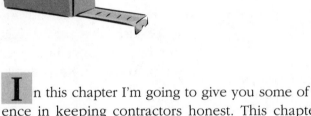

In this chapter I'm going to give you some of my 15 years of experience in keeping contractors honest. This chapter will concentrate on honest and fair pricing. Chapter 2 detailed the process of screening and selecting contractors. This one expands on the selection process and details steps you can take to insure you're getting a fair bid.

First, we'll discuss what's fair. Then I'll direct you to the places you can find sample pricing. Entire reference books are written with actual pricing. You can take such a book and find very detailed pricing information. For example, you can determine the exact cost of what material and labor should run for a 2" x 6" x 14' rafter and installation. I'll discuss these books and let you know what I like about them, and what I don't. Then I'll cover some of the methods I've used over the years to get fair pricing and finally summarize with a list of points from the chapter.

All in all, there are many things you should be doing and checking to insure you get accurate and fair pricing. Notice the word accurate. I think accurate pricing is as important, if not more important, than fair pricing. Most problems I see arising between homeowner and contractor result from the misunderstanding of information that was shared between the two parties. The contractor failed to get everyone on the same page and, with different views, the situation is set on fire. I'll provide you with some tips for avoiding misunderstanding and provide some information that you should make sure you have before you begin your project.

Lack of detail causes more problems than any other on a jobsite. It goes back to the old saying that you can't have too much information. I don't know about other areas of life, but I know this statement is very true in construction. I've learned that added detail solves problems before they begin. I'll outline some ways you can use to insure you not only get fair pricing on bids, but that you keep from getting taken advantage of after the project has begun by including all the necessary information for your situation. First, let's talk about what makes a bid fair.

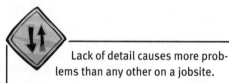

Entire reference books are written with actual pricing. You can take such a book and find very detailed pricing information.

Lack of detail causes more problems than any other on a jobsite.

FAIR BIDS, BUT FAIR TO WHOM?

What makes a price fair? Is the lowest price fair? What about the highest one? What do I even mean by fair? Before you can determine whether a price is fair or not, you have to know what makes a bid fair. Once you know what makes it fair, it's easy to see if it's unfair.

The following points should be met by a bid that's fair. All fair bids will follow these guidelines. If your estimate from the contractor fails to meet even one of them, be cautious. Notice I didn't say throw it out. He should merely have a good, and believable, reason for failing to meet the criteria 100%. You should inquire as to why his bid doesn't cover the missing point. He should provide you with a sound reason. Let's talk about the points that make up a fair price:

- **Fair to all parties.** That's right, all parties. I have fallen prey to only looking out for myself, and I've gotten burned for doing so. For a project to run successfully without major problems, the price has to be fair for everyone. I've taken the bid that I've known to be too low for the job, thinking I was going to save money, and on occasion I have come out alright. However, more often than not, I get burned before all the work's done. I'll elaborate on this more in the upcoming bulleted items. For now, remember all parties include: you, the contractor, his employees, subcontractors, and suppliers. Everyone must be taken care of with fairness, first and foremost.

- **Covers all necessary work.** To be fair, all work must be included in the bid. Check with your contractor when you're reviewing his bid to insure all necessities are covered. You don't want to get unexpected bills for items not covered by the bid. When I'm signing a contract with a homeowner, I try and go over all of their responsibilities - including costs - before we sign. I want no surprises for them or for me. Make sure your estimate includes everything necessary from the permit fee to the final clean up.

- **Accounts for determinable scenarios.** Don't take a price that leaves issues to future discovery unless it's absolutely necessary. For example, don't let a roofer leave sheathing off his bid (because he has to remove your existing shingles before he can see it) if he can get into your attic and look at it from there. For another example, don't let a contractor leave items off his bid until he finds out how long it's going to take to do something. He should know how long it will take or he shouldn't be in this business. It's best to determine as much as you can up front, to eliminate surprises later.

- Covers all necessary insurance. If you have a contractor who gives you a better deal because he pays his men cash or he doesn't carry insurance, run for the hills. This is not acceptable and puts you as the homeowner at great risk. Sure, you can take a risk, and maybe save some dollars, but you could also end up losing big. Take my advice, and make sure the contractor is making enough money to pay for the proper insurance.

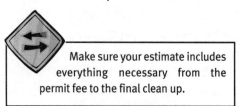

For a project to run successfully without major problems, the price has to be fair for everyone.

- **Allows the contractor to make money.** You want your contractor to make money off you. I know this doesn't sound logical to everyone out there, but it's very true. If your contractor doesn't make money, he won't stay in business. And if he doesn't stay in business, who are you going to call if you have a warranty problem? If your contractor goes out of business because he didn't make any money, your problem will be your problem. You want a financially secure contractor who'll be around if you need him.

Make sure your estimate includes everything necessary from the permit fee to the final clean up.

If you have a contractor who gives you a better deal because he pays his men cash or he doesn't carry insurance, run for the hills.

While you should try and be fair in all your dealings, being fair with your contractor can be self-serving. You'll wind up happier, and possibly richer, in the end by avoiding costly problems. So, first and foremost, be fair. Now let's look at why you should look for sample pricing and where you can find it.

SAMPLE PRICING

As a stated before, entire books are dedicated to sample pricing. These books detail pricing for construction activities listing average costs per man hour and what materials should cost per job. I'll discuss them so you can get a feel for how they work and how to use them.

For your pricing to be fair to you and your contractor, you should follow the advice listed in this section closely. It's amazing how a simple step - either done or undone - can save, or cost, so much money in a small amount of time.

FIGURE 10-1
Books contain sample pricing figures on average situations such as the house in this picture. They can not allow for special considerations. Compare this roof to the one in Figure 10-2.

FIGURE 10-2
This roof has no room for workers on this side of the house. The special considerations needed cannot be estimated by a one-situation-fits-all book.

Where and Why

First, what is sample pricing? Sample pricing is mainly obtained from very thick and expensive books that are written for people like contractors and insurance estimators. It gives them a reference to use when they're bidding work for their customers. They use them for differing reasons.

The contractor wants to charge as much as he can for his work without overpricing for his market. The insurance estimator wants to ensure his company isn't overpaying for repair or replacement work. In short, they both want to charge, or be charged, what is usual and customary for the work being performed.

The books that contain this information are filled with details about figuring the price of work. It breaks down the pricing to many categories of work, and then into subcategories. While this works well for the professional, because he knows how many rafters it takes to frame in a 12' x 16' sun porch roof, it leaves most homeowners in the dark. These books are designed for the individual with an in-depth knowledge of the profession. The layman will have a hard time deciphering all the information needed to arrive at accurate pricing.

> Pricing guides are designed for the individual with an in-depth knowledge of the profession. The layman will have a hard time deciphering all the information needed to arrive at accurate pricing.

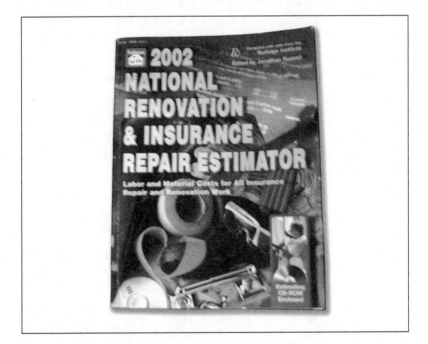

FIGURE 10.3
Sample estimating guide

If these books contain the information, but most home-owners can't understand them and are not willing to pay the high price tag for the books to begin with, what good are they to you? If you don't know what a ridge beam is and why it needs to be load-bearing in a vaulted ceiling, the pricing guides will probably be no good.

I've tried to give you practical information without telling you to go buy an $80 book you probably won't understand anyway. Heck, I've been doing this for 16 years, I'm writing this book, and I get lost in my estimating book sometimes! But, to be safe, I'm going to tell you where you can find this type of book, if you're so inclined, and why I think they're good and bad.

- **Where can I find sample pricing?** Sample pricing can be found in many books available on the market today - see Figure 10-3 for an example. These books are very detailed, costly, and are written mainly for professionals in the construction and insurance industries.

- **Why should I find sample pricing?** If you don't have a clue as to what something should cost, these books can help you establish a starting point to give you some idea of pricing. They can also give you a reference to compare bids. If your estimates seem high, but they're relatively close, you can check to see if you're getting overcharged by checking the contractor's figures against the figures in the book.

- **Can I really get an accurate price from a book?** Yes and no. If you know exactly what's going to done, and exactly how it's going to be done, you can look up every item of work needed and arrive at an accurate figure. However, most homeowners lack the in-depth knowledge needed to arrive at an accurate figure. Plus, every situation is different. These books simply cannot cover all circumstances. In abnormal situations, they can even be misleading by failing to "recognize" the special circumstances that must be accounted for, and therefore charged for. I had never used an estimating book until the last few years while at my current job. I think they're at best a guideline to use for ballpark figures. See Figures 10-1 and 10-2 for two roofs that are very similar to one another; however the circumstances of one make it much different to work on than the other. And subsequently, the price for re-roofing each house is very different even though the actual roofs are very similar to one another.

In my opinion, home-owners should leave estimating books to the people that do the estimating. There are so many other ways to check on pricing, and keep your contractor honest, than killing yourself trying to estimate your own job with one of these thick and confusing books.

> These books simply can not cover all circumstances. In abnormal situations, they can even be misleading by failing to "recognize" the special circumstances that must be accounted for and charged.

The next two sections of this chapter will outline some of these tips so you can check your bids for fairness. Read them well before you get bids on any projects you're contemplating.

Keeping Them Honest

We've covered the hard way to get sample pricing. Now let's talk about some easy common-sense ways to keep your pricing fair and honest. You'll want to insure you follow my advice whenever you're getting bids on a project. In fact, they're good rules to live by whenever you can.

Why is it that we only get multiple bids when we're having some construction done? Why don't we get three bids when we go to our mechanic? Most of us get a price and say OK. Or worse yet, we let the work get done, then wait for the big bomb after it's too late to change anything! I suggest that, whenever possible, you do a little comparison shopping. But, in this book, I'm talking about construction. And in particular, decks, patios, and porches. So, let's talk about them.

I'm going to discuss four tips you should follow anytime it's possible and practical. Don't let excuses stop you from doing the right thing. Getting in a hurry and skipping these points can and will cost you lots of money. Don't do it. Read on and follow my advice to keep yourself protected.

Get Three and Maybe More

Get at least three estimates. And if you don't feel comfortable with the results, get more. Most contractors provide free estimates. Take them up on their offer and have them estimate for you. This is the easiest and best way to insure you get fair pricing. I'll go into this in more detail in Chapter 11. For now, just know you want many estimates to compare to keep your potential contractors honest.

> Get at least three estimates. And if you don't feel comfortable with the results, get more. Most contractors provide free estimates. Take them up on their offer and have them estimate for you.

Details, Details, Details

Make your estimators include as much detail as you can think of in their estimates. If you get an estimate with only the basics, be very leery. The estimate may be completely devoid of details. What brand of materials is being used? What are the specifications? How long is the warranty on the product and the workmanship? You want your estimates to include as much detailed information as possible.

> You want your estimates to include as much detailed information as possible.

Extras Cost Money

Make sure your contractor has included all the necessary work in his estimate. You don't want him to come back later with an additional bill because something wasn't included in the esti-mate. Make sure they include everything that needs done to complete the job from start to finish. It should include every-thing from the permit fees to the initial clean-up fees and everything in between. Don't let them come back on you for more money once they've started. To accomplish this, you have to ask questions before any work begins (while he's esti-mating is best) not after you sign a contract and he's started.

Changes Are Bad

Many contractors make a lot of money on changes. This means you can't make unnecessary changes after you begin. Don't decide to move the built-in benches from your deck to the west side, instead of the east side, after they're installed. The time to move things around is while they're still on paper, not on your new deck. Many contractors will charge premium amounts for any changes you make them go through. Don't give your contractor an excuse to jab you; stick to the original plan.

Follow these guidelines to help keep your potential and actual contractors honest and your pricing fair. Anyone can follow these simple guidelines without buying an expensive book and without having in-depth knowledge of construction.

Common sense and practical answers have always worked best for me. I try and treat my customers and my subcontrac-tors by the golden rule. I treat them well, as I would like to be treated. And for the most part, this rule has served me well. I get good pricing from my subs and I get happy customers when their projects are completed.

By using common-sense approaches like I've outlined, you should be able to keep your contractor of choice honest. By following the advice in this book you'll find the con-tractor that's right for you and your project. You'll be able to

> The time to move things around is while they're still on paper, not on your new deck. Many contractors will charge premium amounts for any changes you request after the work is in progress.

weed out the ones that want to overcharge or undercharge for their services, and choose the best one for you.

SUMMARY

Use the easy methods outlined in this chapter to obtain fair pricing on your next project. You don't have to know what a collar tie is to decipher what's fair and what's not. It's a simple matter of comparison. To summarize, here's a list of the highlights:

- A fair price is fair to all parties involved. This includes the contractor and his workers, as well as you.
- A broke contractor doesn't make warranty repairs. He has to make some money on your project to stay in business.
- Sample pricing books are better left to the pros. Follow my common-sense checks instead.
- Get three or more estimates every time.
- Include details, details, and more details on your estimates.
- Make sure all work is bid to avoid extra charges by your contractor.

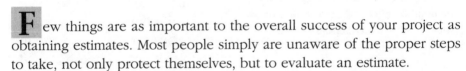

11

The Bidding Process When Seeking a Contractor

Few things are as important to the overall success of your project as obtaining estimates. Most people simply are unaware of the proper steps to take, not only protect themselves, but to evaluate an estimate.

Evaluating what you have is very important. Most people simply take the low bidder, without looking at other aspects of the situation. There are many points to be considered when obtaining bids. In fact, there is a whole process that should be followed that will almost guarantee success. I'm going to discuss those steps in this chapter. Read the information carefully. This is one of the most critical steps in the process.

OBTAINING AND DECIPHERING ESTIMATES

When it comes to estimates, they come in all shapes and sizes. The key is to get your contractors all on the same page so they're bidding the same thing. You want them all bidding the same size structure with the same materials and features. You can't compare bids that aren't bidding the same thing. It's your job to make sure all your contractors know exactly what they're bidding so you wind up with multiple bids for the same structure - including all the little details.

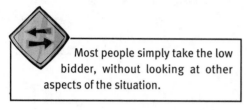

Most people simply take the low bidder, without looking at other aspects of the situation.

You can't control the format of the estimates you'll be getting. They'll surely be as varied as your contractors themselves. But to make an informed decision, you must control the content in the bid.

Getting Your Project Estimated

Out of the several contractors you've met with (assuming you've read and followed my advice from Chapter 2), choose

The key is to get your contractors all on the same page so they're bidding the same thing. You want them all bidding the same size structure with the same materials and features.

at least three. If you've cut your list to less than three, start over until you have at least three that make it this far. You want to have these three give you a formal estimate.

You should have enough information to choose a single project, or at worst two pos-

sible projects to compare, before having your potential contractors give you written estimates.

Check with the contractors you've chosen to see if they provide free estimates. Most contractors don't charge for this service, but some do. If they do, have them quote the fee, then decide if you want to pay it or not. Find out why they charge a fee. Decide if they're charging a small nominal fee to weed out customers who aren't serious about their projects, or if they're trying to turn a buck while bidding your job. The former is acceptable; the latter is not.

If you do pay for an estimate, you should always negotiate the cost of the estimate out of the final price. After all, he was only trying to avoid unnecessary bidding, not trying to make money from bidding. Therefore, the cost of your estimate should be refunded in the job.

Contact the selected bidders and lay out what you want estimated. They may or may not want to revisit your home. If they've taken enough information with them from your pre-bid meeting (discussed in Chapter 2), they shouldn't need to. If

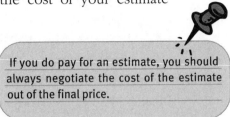

If you do pay for an estimate, you should always negotiate the cost of the estimate out of the final price.

you have special considerations, make sure you outline them so each contractor will bid the same work. For example, you have to move your air conditioning condenser from its current location to the side of the house so it won't be next to your deck. Make sure each contractor knows to include this work in their estimate. You can't be too specific when you outline what you want from your contractors. You should include all of the following information:

- What type of structure you want. If you have pictures from magazines, make sure your contractors have seen them.

- The structure's dimensions. This should include depth for concrete patios.

- Specific materials to be estimated including types of: screening, roofing, soffit, fascia, doors, windows, and other material to be estimated.

- Structural design features (if you know them) including: footing depth and size, joist size, flooring size, rafter size, sheathing requirements, etc.

- Finish design features including: color, textures, patterns, rail detail, ceiling detail, and specific finish materials to be estimated.

- Special considerations such as: utilities to be relocated, fixtures to be relocated or removed, and electrical, HVAC or plumbing to be estimated.

- Any other specific instructions you want followed. Maybe as you don't want your redbud tree damaged because your husband planted it on your 5th wedding anniversary.

You want all of your estimates to include all of the same items and all of the same work. To make a fair assessment, you need to be comparing apples to apples.

If there are details you haven't quite made your mind up about, have the estimators give you an allowance. For example, you haven't yet decided what type of siding you want on your screen room. Have your contractors give you an allowance for siding materials and labor. This way, all your bids will be the same and, if you choose a different siding, you just substitute the new material and installation price for the old one.

Set a timetable for estimates to be sent to you. This can usually be done within two weeks. Let the bidders know you want the estimates in your hand by _____. Now fill in the blank with a date and time. Make sure the date is agreeable to all parties involved.

How they get the bids to you isn't important. It's their job to get them to you. They can hand deliver them, mail them, fax them, or e-mail them; it doesn't matter to you. It's their job to figure this out. Your job is to receive them and review them after the deadline, or once you have them all in hand. Don't accept late bids. You've set a deadline and all parties agreed to it. If a contractor can't meet a simple bid deadline, do you think he'll meet other deadlines?

> If there are details you haven't quite made your mind up about, have the estimators give you an allowance.

Reviewing and Comparing Estimates

Once you've received all your estimates, it's time to review them. You want to read everything that's written on them, and everything that's not. You also want to decipher all the nonwritten hints. These hints give you insight into each contractor's habits and business practices.

To make the right decision, you have to look at more than the bottom line. The best-priced bid isn't always the best deal. There's more to consider than the bottom line.

You'll want to look at the format and detail of the estimate as well. Take each estimate out and lay them side by side on your desk or kitchen table. Now check them each against the following criteria:

- Can you easily read the bid and determine what the contractor is proposing to do? Is all the information clear and easy to read?

- Is the contractor's contact information clear? Does it include his company name, address, phone number and fax number? Is the person who completed the bid listed by name on the estimate? From his estimate, would you know who to contact with questions?

- Are all of the prices clear? Can you tell what each price is and what it's for? Is the total price clear?

- Is the estimate detailed? Can you easily tell what they're estimating? Are all your special considerations/conditions listed clearly? Does the estimate spell out exactly what's to be done?

- Is everything itemized? Is there a separation between materials and labor if it's needed? If you requested specific materials, is their use specifically called out in the estimate?

The example in 11-1 is an example of a neat and detailed estimate. The contractor who prepared this estimate took his time and paid attention to detail. He will hopefully take the same time and pay the same attention to detail when working on your project.

After reviewing your estimates, you should have a clear view of which contractor is right for you.

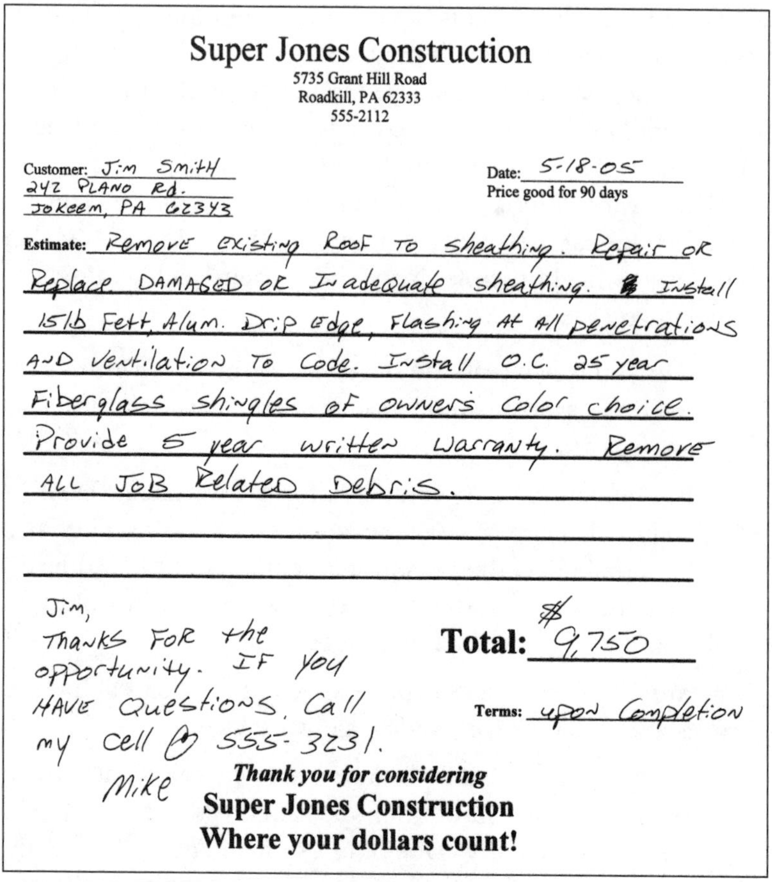

Super Jones Construction
5735 Grant Hill Road
Roadkill, PA 62333
555-2112

Customer: _Jim Smith_
242 PLANO Rd.
Jokeem, PA 62343

Date: _5-18-05_
Price good for 90 days

Estimate: _Remove existing Roof To sheathing. Repair or_
Replace DAMAGED or Inadequate sheathing. Install
15lb Felt, Alum. Drip Edge, Flashing At All penetrations
AND Ventilation To Code. Install O.C. 25 year
Fiberglass shingles of owners Color choice.
Provide 5 year written Warranty. Remove
All JoB Related Debris.

Jim,
Thanks For the
opportunity. IF you
HAVE Questions, Call
my Cell @ 555-3231.
　　　Mike

Total: _$9,750_

Terms: _upon Completion_

Thank you for considering
Super Jones Construction
Where your dollars count!

FIGURE 11-1
This is an example of an orderly estimate.

Consider the total prices from your bids. If you have two or more estimates that are similar in price and one that is much lower or much higher - be leery of the different one. For example, you've asked for estimates for a new deck. Two of your estimates are between $4,000 and $5,000, but the third is much lower or much higher than the other two. Be very careful and ask questions to determine why the third bid is so different. If you don't get solid answers to your questions, and a good explanation as to why it's so much different, discard it.

Usually a much lower, or higher, bid is that way for a reason. The contractor missed materials or labor in his bid, or left something out entirely, or he's just overpriced. None of these scenarios is good.

> If you have two or more estimates that are similar in price and one that is much lower or much higher - be leery of the different one.

While a much lower bid may sound like a great break for you, it's not. If you accept the much lower bid, and the contractor takes the job, you'll lose in the long run. Once he's realized he's going to lose money, your project will suffer. At the very least he'll try and save every penny he can and will rush through your project. He may even try and recoup his lost money with a change order or add-on up charge. None of these scenarios is good for your project. It's best to accept a viable bid and get the job done right the first time.

> While a much lower bid may sound like a great break for you, it's not. If you accept the much lower bid, and the contractor takes the job, you'll lose in the long run.

Accepting the Bid

OK, you've reviewed the bids and you've chosen the one you like. You reviewed it by using all of the information outlined thus far in the chapter, so now all you have to do is call the contractor and say OK. Right? Wrong!

Just because you've decided on a bid, and therefore a contractor, don't think you're done. You still have to check on several things before you can sit back, write checks, and watch the work commence. I'm going to provide you with a list of

Contractor	Appt. Time	Notes: on time, courteous, taking measurements, etc.

FIGURE 11.2
Contractor log

items that need to be verified before you can sit back and relax. Failure to do so can result in disaster.

For your project to run just the way you've worked and dreamed for, you'll have to make sure you and your contractor are on the same page. This means communication. Review the list below and take some notes so you can call your contractor and get his responses to the listed questions.

- **Timing?** You've chosen contractor XYZ, but when can he start on your project? While a good contractor is worth waiting for, you may have a deadline you expect him to meet that he simply can't. You'll have to decide whether to wait for him or not. Keep in mind, that any contractor who's worth his salt should be busy. He will probably not be able to start on your project tomorrow.

You simply want to know when he can start and if you can live with his timing.

- **How long?** He can start in two weeks, great! Right? Well, maybe. The starting time works, but when will he finish? You want a solid end date to your project. Your contract should reflect this date. You also want to know if they'll be working on your project continually once they start, or will they be pulling off your project to work on someone else's? You'll want to see almost continual progress on your job, once it's started, until it's complete.

- **Access.** What parts of your home does the contractor need access to? Where will they store their materials and tools? Do they need access to electric and water, or toilet

FIGURE 11-3
Find out how many trucks your contractor's crews will be driving and where they'll need to park them. Overcrowding can become a problem for you and your neighbors.

facilities? How many trucks will be at your home on a daily basis and where are they going to park? You'll want to cover all aspects of how work will commence and what to expect while the work's being completed.

- **You plan on working when?** Ask what hours your contractor's crews normally work. If you work third shift, and they plan on starting at 5:30 am, will this be a problem? Will they be working any evenings? or weekends? Will the crews be there at 3:00 in the afternoon when your kids get home from school?

- **Insurance binder.** If you didn't request it at the pre-bid meeting, get a copy of your contractor's insurance binder. You should get a hard copy of his insurance, including workman's compensation insurance.

- **Copy of contract.** Ask for a copy of his standard contract so you can review the document. Compare it to the sample contract. Are all of the pertinent information and specific details covered?

> If you didn't request it at the pre-bid meeting, get a copy of your contractor's insurance binder. You should get a hard copy of his insurance, including workman's compensation insurance.

> A contractor who's been in business for any length of time usually will have a lengthy contract.

If you and your winning bidder have covered the above list and everything meets your requirements, it's time to review his contract in detail and get going on your project. Keep in mind; there are as many contracts out there as there are contractors. What you want to be aware of is the basic information is included. I've learned over the years to include as much detail as I possibly can in my contracts. A contractor who's been in business for any length of time usually will have a lengthy contract. A lengthy contract with lots of detail will protect you and your contractor.

SUMMARY

You now know the detailed steps to take during the process of receiving and reviewing estimates. Follow all the steps to insure success on your outdoor project. Don't forget the following points:

- A sloppy bid is a sign of a sloppy contractor.
- The low bidder is not always the best bidder.
- If one of your three estimates is much different from the other two, be very careful and determine why it is so much lower.
- Cover timing and continuous work schedules with your contractor before signing a contract.
- Discuss access to your home, material and tool storage, and parking arrangements with your contractor before signing a contract.

12

Putting It in Writing

Get it in writing! These four words convey the most important message in remodeling. The significance of having everything in writing cannot be stressed enough. Written documents solve problems before they happen and eliminate confusion. Concise written agreements protect your investment and assure your satisfaction. Without these agreements, you are exposed to a variety of uncontrollable, potentially devastating problems.

THE OUTLINE

The first form you will use is the outline. This form gives you the ability to document and organize your intended improvements in writing. No signatures or legal jargon are required in this form. It is simply an orderly list of your desires. A good outline should be arranged in chronological order. The categories create an overview of the scope of the work to be done. The information should focus on of the types of work you want done, not the products you intend to use. If you want to convert a closet or make room for a whirlpool tub, this is where you define the project. This outline will be helpful when you define your anticipated costs.

Keeping a written report of your remodeling interests will make your life simpler. You won't forget to price work in the bidding stage, because the outline reminds you to request quotes. Put everything on the outline. Include the faucets you want replaced, the location of carpets to be installed, and the skylight you are considering. This is not a bid sheet, so put everything you want on it. You can edit the list later. It is only for proposed work.

CONTRACTOR SELECTION FORM

When your outline is complete, move on to the contractor selection form. This form is designed to aid during the contractor selection process. All the major groups of subcontractors are listed on the form, and you should note those you will need on your job. When you get to the bidding process, this list will be very helpful. Knowing which subs to call will be obvious, and omissions are less likely. The contractor selection form can also remind you of a phase of work previously forgotten.

You will know the types of contactors you may need to call, some of which could include:

- Carpenter
- Plumber
- Heating contractor
- Electrician
- Insulator
- Drywall contractor
- Painter
- Wallpaper contractor
- Flooring contractor

CONTRACTOR QUESTIONNAIRE

PLEASE ANSWER ALL THE FOLLOWING QUESTIONS, AND EXPLAIN ANY "NO" ANSWERS.

Company name _____

Physical company address _____

Company mailing address _____

Company phone number _____

After hours phone number _____

Company President/Owner _____

President/Owner address _____

President/Owner phone number _____

How long has company been in business? _____

Name of insurance company _____

Insurance company phone number _____

Does company have liability insurance? _____

Amount of liability insurance coverage _____

Does company have Workman's Comp. insurance? _____

Type of work company is licensed to do _____

List Business or other license numbers _____

Where are licenses held? _____

If applicable, are all workman licensed? _____

Are there any lawsuits pending against the company? _____

Has the company ever been sued? _____

Does the company use subcontractors? _____

Is the company bonded? _____

Who is the company bonded with? _____

Has the company ever had complaints filed against it? _____

Are there any judgments against the company? _____

Please list 3 references of work similar to ours:

#1 _____

#2 _____

#3 _____

Please list 3 credit references:

#1 _____

#2 _____

#3 _____

Please list 3 trade references:

#1 _____

#2 _____

#3 _____

Please note any information you feel will influence our decision:

_____

ALL OF THE ABOVE INFORMATION IS TRUE AND ACCURATE AS OF THIS DATE.

DATE:_____   COMPANY NAME: _____

BY:_____   TITLE: _____

CONTRACTOR RATING SHEET

Job name: _____   Date: _____

Category	Contractor 1	Contractor 2	Contractor 3
Contractor name			
Returns calls			
Licensed			
Insured			
Bonded			
References			
Price			
Experience			
Years in business			
Work quality			
Availability			
Deposit required			
Detailed quote			
Personality			
Punctual			
Gut reaction			

Notes: _____

_____

_____

_____

_____

_____

_____

CONTRACTOR SELECTION FORM

TYPE OF SERVICE	VENDOR NAME	PHONE NUMBER	DATE SCHEDULED
Site Work	N/A		
Footings	N/A		
Concrete	N/A		
Foundation	N/A		
Waterproofing	N/A		
Masonry	N/A		
Framing	J. P. Buildal	231-8294	7/3/04
Roofing	N/A		
Siding	N/A		
Exterior Trim	N/A		
Gutters	N/A		
Pest Control	N/A		
Plumbing/R-I	TMG Plumbing, Inc.	242-1987	7/9/04
HVAC/R-I	Warming's HVAC	379-9071	7/15/04
Electrical/R-I	Bright Electric	257-2225	7/18/04
Central Vacuum	N/A		
Insulation	Allstar Insulators	242-4792	7/24/04
Drywall	Hank's Drywall	379-6638	7/29/04
Painter	J. C. Brush	247-8931	8/15/04
Wallpaper	N/A		
Tile	N/A		
Cabinets	N/A		
Countertops	N/A		
Interior Trim	The Final Touch Co.	365-1962	8/8/04
Floor Covering	Carpet Magicians	483-8724	8/19/04
Plumbing/Final	Same	Same	8/21/04
HVAC/Final	Same	Same	8/22/04
Electrical/Final	Same	Same	8/23/04
Cleaning	N/A		
Paving	N/A		
Landscaping	N/A		

NOTES/CHANGES _____

This form serves as a reminder of which trades will be needed to complete the work. You will need competitive bids for each phase of the job to plan your budget. A budget loses its effectiveness if you forget that you will need a tile contractor for your bathroom remodel. There are spaces on the form to list the name and phone number of the company you choose to do each phase of work. This allows you to use the form as a quick reference sheet during the project. The more you have in writing, the less you will forget.

QUERY LETTER

Your next written tool will be the Query Letter, which requests prices and inquires about the availability of services. Mailing this form letter to all the professionals you anticipate needing will save you time and money. The letter saves hours of phone calls to answering services.

Mailed requests for information are an effective way to cover all the bases. You can send a letter to every contractor in the phone book and eliminate days of phone calls.

Form letters allow you to achieve maximum results with minimal effort. They are effective with professionals, contractors, and suppliers alike. Written requests for service rates, material prices, and availability will eliminate disinterested parties. A form letter saves you untold time in wasted phone calls. Companies that respond to your letter will be eager for your business. These companies offer the best opportunity for good service and low prices.

PRODUCT INFORMATION SHEET

The next form you will need is the product identification sheet. This sheet is divided into construction phases. It will detail all the specifics of the products you are interested in. The sheet lists information such as:

- Brand name
- Model number
- Color
- Size
- Other pertinent information

Do you feel like you are being buried in paperwork? These forms don't have to be used, but the results without them are unpredictable at best. At this point you know the work

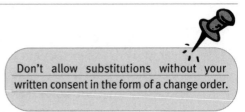

Don't allow substitutions without your written consent in the form of a change order.

you want done and the people required to do it. You even have your product list ready for bids. Are you ready to start the job? No, there is still work to be done in the office before the fieldwork is started.

ESTIMATED COST SHEET

Review the information you have assembled. Create files for all the suppliers and contractors. These files will help you during your negotiations and final decision. Using an estimated cost sheet is the next logical approach. This worksheet will give you a rough idea of the costs required to complete your home improvement project. The estimate sheet will be divided into phases of work, such as:

- Framing

- Siding

- Trim

- Electrical

- HVAC

- Plumbing

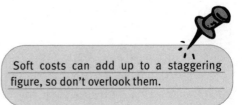

Soft costs can add up to a staggering figure, so don't overlook them.

These phases are considered hard costs. In addition, your estimated cost sheet should include soft costs. These are professional fees, loan application fees, interest charges, and other broad-based costs.

The estimated cost sheet should include all expenses. You have to know what the total cash requirements will be before committing to a project. If you forget to include soft costs, you could run out of money before the job is finished. Review the sample cost sheets and add categories as needed. Some hidden expenses could be related to a home- improvement loan. These loans can require points, title searches, application fees, closing costs, and other financial expenses. Be aware of these potential costs and allow for them in your estimate.

FINE-TUNING THE PRELIMINARY DESIGN

With your estimating done, you can move on to the next step. This involves fine- tuning your preliminary design. Refer to the specifications sheet you have created. It should detail all the proposed materials for the job. It is time to begin to cross-reference the information in the stack of paperwork you have generated. The specifications sheet should be accompanied by a revised contractor list. Perhaps you found that you cannot afford a stone fireplace or quarry tile floor. These changes need to be reflected in your spec sheet. Adjust the estimated remodeling costs in accordance with your proposed changes. At this stage you are getting ready to get final quotes.

The changes you make within the specifications sheet may affect your contractor selection list. Changing the scope of the work may eliminate the need for some subcontractors. Make these notations on your contractor selection form. Don't waste time contacting contractors you don't need.

Every job should start with good written agreements and a strong production plan. Predicting an accurate financial budget is vital to completing a successful job.

BID REQUEST FORM

The bidding process is the financial backbone of your job. A Bid Request Form is an intricate part of the bidding process. Without it, you are dealing with ambiguous, bulk numbers.

CONTRACTOR QUESTIONNAIRE

When you are ready to start making commitments, you need to tie down the details. A contractor questionnaire can help with this important procedure. Some questions to ask potential contractors include:

- Do the contractors you plan to use have liability insurance?
- Do they provide worker's compensation insurance for their employees?
- Are their workers properly licensed?
- Does the contractor have the required business licenses?
- Is the contractor licensed to do the work you are requesting?
- Will the work performed be done by employees or subcontractors?
- Is the contractor bonded?
- Have the contractors and subcontractors ever had complaints filed against them by other customers?

These are questions you should answer before signing a contract. The questionnaire is designed to ask these questions without embarrassing you. When a contractor is asked to complete a form, they know you are requesting the same information from other contractors. This competition will provide the motivation for the contractor to answer the questions. The form also gives you the opportunity to get a contractor's answers in writing.

It is easy for a remodeler to side-step your verbal questions or even to answer the questions with lies. Questionable contractors will think twice before answering with lies in writing; they could be charged with fraud. This is a proven way to cull the crop of bad contractors. Don't feel bad about asking them to complete this form. If they are good contractors, they will have no problem answering the questions in writing. The bad ones will disappear and save you a lot of trouble.

CONTRACTS

Once you find the right contractors, you are ready to proceed with your contracts. There is no reason to limit written contracts to tradespeople. While it not a routine business practice to contract with suppliers, it is a good idea. You can achieve additional assurances of your prices and delivery dates with a solid contract. Don't be afraid to ask for a contract from everyone involved in the project. Everything you have in writing reduces your risks.

A written contract with your general contractor or subcontractors is absolutely necessary. Contracts are an accepted requirement in building and remodeling. The contract should be strict but fair.

A written contract is the last word in your job. It answers all the questions and calls all the shots. The contract is for your benefit, and you should have some input in its structure. Don't leave the contract preparation in the hands of a lawyer without providing your personal input. Lawyers know law, but they don't necessarily know remodeling or your needs and desires. And, if you encounter a contractor who is in breech of contract, serve formal notice of the breech.

If you slant a contract too heavily to your advantage, contractors will not sign it. Most contractors will want you to sign their proposal or contract. They will have pre-printed forms, with the information regarding your job filled in the blank spaces. Contracts ultimately protect those who write them, so try to avoid using a contract supplied by others. Contractors may resist at first, but they will sign your contract if it's fair.

Now it's done; you have all your contracts signed. You probably thought you would never see the end of the paperwork. Well, you haven't; the job is only about to begin. There are reams of paper yet to be used. A successful job runs on paper. Without it you

Legal documents such as contracts should be prepared by attorneys. Attorneys have the skill and knowledge to write contracts capable of standing the test of the courts.

Your Company Name
Your Company Address
Your Company Phone and Fax Numbers

SUBCONTRACTOR AGREEMENT

This agreement, made this _____ day of _____, 20__, shall set forth the whole agreement, in its entirety, between Contractor and Subcontractor.

Contractor: _____, referred to herein as Contractor.

Job location: _____

Subcontractor: _____, referred to herein as Subcontractor.

The Contractor and Subcontractor agree to the following.

SCOPE OF WORK

Subcontractor shall perform all work as described below and provide all material to complete the work described below.

Subcontractor shall supply all labor and material to complete the work according to the attached plans and specifications. These attached plans and specifications have been initialed and signed by all parties. The work shall include, but is not limited to, the following: _____

_____

_____

_____

_____

COMMENCEMENT AND COMPLETION SCHEDULE

The work described above shall be started within _____ (____) days of verbal notice from Contractor, the projected start date is _____.
The Subcontractor shall complete the above work in a professional and expedient manner by no later than _____ (____) days from the start date. Time is of the essence in this contract. No extension of time will be valid without the Contractor's written consent. If Subcontractor does not complete the work in the time allowed, and if the lack of completion is not caused by the Contractor, the Subcontractor will be charged _____ ($_____) dollars per day, for every day work extends beyond the completion date. This charge will be deducted from any payments due to the Subcontractor for work performed.

(Page 1 of 3. Please initial _____.)

SUBCONTRACTOR AGREEMENT (continued)

CONTRACT SUM

The Contractor shall pay the Subcontractor for the performance of completed work subject to additions and deductions as authorized by this agreement or attached addendum. The contract sum is

_____($_____).

PROGRESS PAYMENTS

The Contractor shall pay the Subcontractor installments as detailed below, once an acceptable insurance certificate has been filed by the Subcontractor with the Contractor. Contractor shall pay the Subcontractor as described: _____

   All payments are subject to a site inspection and approval of work by the Contractor. Before final payment, the Subcontractor shall submit satisfactory evidence to the Contractor that no lien risk exists on the subject property.

WORKING CONDITIONS

Working hours will be _____ a.m. through _____ p.m., Monday through Friday. Subcontractor is required to clean work debris from the job site on a daily basis and leave the site in a clean and neat condition. Subcontractor shall be responsible for removal and disposal of all debris related to the job description.

CONTRACT ASSIGNMENT

Subcontractor shall not assign this contract or further subcontract the whole of this subcontract, without the written consent of the Contractor.

LAWS, PERMITS, FEES, AND NOTICES

Subcontractor shall be responsible for all required laws, permits, fees, or notices, required to perform the work stated herein.

WORK OF OTHERS

Subcontractor shall be responsible for any damage caused to existing conditions or other contractor's work. This damage will be repaired, and the Subcontractor charged for the expense and supervision of this work. The Subcontractor shall have the opportunity to quote a price for said repairs, but the Contractor is under no obligation to engage the Subcontractor to make said repairs. If a different subcontractor repairs the damage, the Subcontractor may be back charged for the cost of the repairs. Any repair costs will be deducted from any payments due to the Subcontractor. If no payments are due the Subcontractor, the Subcontractor shall pay the invoiced amount within _____ (_____) days.

(Page 2 of 3. Please initial _____.)

SUBCONTRACTOR AGREEMENT (continued)

WARRANTY

Subcontractor warrants to the Contractor, all work and materials for
_____ from the final day of work performed.

INDEMNIFICATION

To the fullest extent allowed by law, the Subcontractor shall indemnify and
hold harmless the Owner, the Contractor, and all of their agents and
employees from and against all claims, damages, losses, and expenses.

This agreement, entered into on _____, 20_____, shall
constitute the whole agreement between Contractor and Subcontractor.

_____   _____
Contractor   Date   Subcontractor   Date

(Page 3 of 3)

Your Company Name
Your Company Address
Your Company Phone and Fax Numbers

SUBCONTRACTOR CONTRACT ADDENDUM

This addendum is an integral part of the contract dated
_____, between the Contractor, _____,
and the Customer(s), _____, for
the work being done on real estate commonly known as _____.

The undersigned parties hereby agree to the following:
_____
_____
_____
_____

The above constitutes the only additions to the above-mentioned contract.
No verbal agreements or other changes shall be valid unless made in
writing and signed by all parties.

_____   _____
Contractor   Date   Customer   Date

                                   _____
                                   Customer   Date

Your Company Name
Your Company Address
Your Company Phone and Fax Numbers

NOTICE OF BREACH OF CONTRACT

Date: _____

To: _____   From: _____

_____   _____

_____   _____

TAKE NOTICE that under Contract made _____, 20 _____, as evidenced by the following documents: _____, we are hereby holding you IN BREACH for the following reasons: _____

_____

_____

_____

If your Breach is not cured within _____ days (i.e., cure must be completed by _____, 20 _____), we will take all further actions necessary to mitigate our damages and protect our rights, which may include, but are not necessarily limited to, the right to Cover" by obtaining substitute performance and chargeback to you of all additional costs and damages incurred.

This Notice is made under the Uniform Commercial Code (if applicable) and all other applicable laws. All rights are hereby reserved, none of which are waived. Any forbearance or temporary waiver from enforcement shall not constitute permanent waiver or waiver of any other right.

You are urged to cure your Breach forthwith.

_____

Contractor

By: _____

Authorized Signatory

will suffer in the end. What else could you possibly need to put in writing? Some suggestions include, change orders, lien waivers, and completion certificates.

CHANGE ORDER

Once the job is started, it is sure to produce unexpected results. When these problems arise, you need to adapt your plans and agreements to accommodate any necessary changes. Use a written change order for every deviation from the contract. You must maintain consistency in your construction management. Written change orders reinforce your dedication to have every aspect of the work clearly defined in black and white.

During the job, you will be tempted to avoid all of this paperwork, especially change orders. You will gain a comfort level with your contractors, which will make change orders seem unnecessary. If you get a phone call at the office regarding mandatory alterations, you will be tempted to give verbal authorization for changes over the phone. Resist these urges. If the situation demands immediate verbal authorization, follow it up with a change order as soon as possible. It is important to maintain continuity. If you start making exceptions, your paperwork will become almost useless.

Contractors will be less likely to take advantage of you when change orders are used, and there will be fewer misunderstandings. Requiring the use of written change orders prevents unexpected price increases. Your contract should mention that change orders will be required for any changes or additional work. In this way a contractor is not entitled to payment for extra work unless you first authorize it in writing. By requiring written change orders, you will be better prepared if you find yourself in court.

CODE COMPLIANCE FORMS

As work progresses, contractors will want to be paid. In most cases, local code- enforcement inspections will be required

Your Company Name
Your Company Address
Your Company Phone and Fax Number

CHANGE ORDER

This change order is an integral part of the contract dated_____,
between the customer _____, and the contractor,
_____, for the work to be
performed. The job location is _____. The following changes are
the only changes to be made. These changes shall now become a part of
the original contract and may not be altered again without written
authorization from all parties.
Changes to be as follows:

_____
_____
_____
_____
_____

These changes will increase / decrease the original contract amount.
Payment for theses changes will be made as follows:
_____. The amount of
change in the contract price will be
_____ ($_____). The new total
contract price shall be _____
($_____).

The undersigned parties hereby agree that these are the only changes to
be made to the original contract. No verbal agreements will be valid. No
further alterations will be allowed without additional written authorization,
signed by all parties. This change order constitutes the entire agreement
between the parties to alter the original contract.

_____   _____
Customer   Contractor

_____   _____
Date   Date

_____
Customer

_____
Date

CODE VIOLATION NOTIFICATION

CUSTOMER NAME: Mr. & Mrs. J. P. Homeowner
CUSTOMER ADDRESS: 192 Hometown Street
CUSTOMER CITY/STATE/ZIP: Ourtown, MO 00580
CUSTOMER PHONE NUMBER: (000) 555-1212
JOB LOCATION: Same
DATE: July 25, 2004
TYPE OF WORK: Electrical
CONTRACTOR: Flashy Electrical Service
ADDRESS: 689 Walnut Ridge, Boltz, MO 00580

OFFICIAL NOTIFICATION OF CODE VIOLATIONS

On July 24, 2004, I was notified by the local electrical code enforcement officer of code violations in the work performed by your company. The violations must be corrected within two business days, as per our contract dated July 1, 2004. Please contact the codes officer for a detailed explanation of the violations and required corrections. If the violations are not corrected within the allotted time, you may be penalized, as per our contract, for your actions, delaying the completion of this project. Thank you for your prompt attention to this matter.

_____   _____
J. P. Homeowner   Date

on the work done. Don't advance any payments until these inspections are completed and accepted. The codes office will provide written evidence of satisfactory inspections. Insist on a copy of each inspection certificate from the contractor. This protects you from code-violation problems. If a code officer turns down an inspection, complete a code violation notification and give it to the appropriate contractor. This notification gives the contractor a specific period of time to have the work corrected and approved by the code officer. In this way you avoid delays, which may affect other trades and throw your project way off schedule. Stipulate in the contract your desire for a photocopy of all permits and inspection results.

> Going to court is never a planned part of remodeling. It is an activity you want to avoid. The best way to bypass the courts is to maintain clear, concise, written agreements.

LIEN WAVER FORM

Before paying anyone, you should complete a lien waiver form. One of these should be signed by any vendor receiving money for services or materials related to your job. Require the lien waiver to be signed at the time you make payment for the service or material. The lien waiver is like your receipt for issuing payment and will protect your home from mechanic's and materialman's liens.

> Never advance money to a contractor until the work passes the inspection of the local code officer.

PUNCH LIST

A punch list is a written notice to contractors of items left to be completed or repaired. These lists come into play at the end of the job. When contractors are finished, you should inspect all the work before final payment is made. Use the punch list form to note all unsatisfactory or incomplete workmanship or materials. After your inspection and before final payment, present a copy of the punch list to the contractor. Have the contractor agree to the list by signing it and allow a reasonable time for corrections to be made. When the punch work is done, inspect the job again. If there are still deficiencies, complete another punch list. Continue this process until the work is done to your satisfaction.

Here is some advice about the proper usage of the punch list:

- Remember that, throughout the remodeling process, we have stressed the need to be fair.

- Be realistic about the work you demand on the punch list.

- Don't require the contractor to replace an entire roll of wallpaper just because there is a tiny wrinkle down by the floor.

- Do not allow a contractor to bully you into accepting work with obvious or offensive flaws.

- Be very thorough when you make the first punch list. Contractors will be quickly angered if they repair everything on your list only to have you find additional items that you missed in your initial inspection.

- Only add items to the list that were caused by the punch work.

You can use a retainer system when dealing with a punch list. Your contractor will want some payment before doing the punch list, and this is okay. But make sure that you retain enough money to pay some other contractor if necessary to have the problems corrected.

CERTIFICATE OF COMPLETION

Certificates of completion document the conclusion dates of all work performed. This form is important in determining your warranty period. Contractors normally offer one-year warranties on their work, and the manufacturer's warranty applies

SAMPLE CERTIFICATE OF COMPLETION AND ACCEPTANCE

CONTRACTOR: _Willy's Drywall Service_

CUSTOMER: _David R Erastus_

JOB NAME: _Erastus_

JOB LOCATION: _134 Faye Lane, Beau, VA 29999_

JOB DESCRIPTION: _Supply and install drywall in new addition, as per plans and specifications, and as described in the contract dated, 6/10/04, between the two parties. Hang, tape, sand, and prepare wall and ceiling surfaces for paint._

DATE OF COMPLETION: _August 13, 2004_

DATE OF FINAL INSPECTION BY CUSTOMER: _August 13, 2004_

DATE OF CODE COMPLIANCE INSPECTION & APPROVAL: _August 13, 2004_

ANY DEFICIENCIES FOUND BY CUSTOMER: _None_

NOTE ANY DEFECTS IN MATERIAL OR WORKMANSHIP: _None_

ACKNOWLEDGEMENT

Customer acknowledges the completion of all contracted work and accepts all workmanship and materials as being satisfactory. Upon signing this certificate, the customer releases the contractor from any responsibility for additional work, except warranty work. Warranty work will be performed for a period of one year from August 13, 2004. Warranty work will include the repair of any material or workmanship defects occurring after this date. All existing workmanship and materials are acceptable to the customer and payment will be made, in full, according to the payment schedule in the contract, between the two parties.

_____   _____

Customer   Date   Contractor   Date

SAMPLE DAMAGE CLAUSE

CONTRACTOR LIABILITY FOR DAMAGES TO EXISTING CONDITIONS

Contractor shall be responsible for any damage caused to existing conditions. This shall include work performed on the project by other contractors. If the contractor damages existing conditions or work performed by other contractors, said contractor shall be responsible for the repair of said damages. These repairs may be made by the contractor responsible for the damages or another contractor, at the discretion of the homeowner.

If a different contractor repairs the damage, the contractor causing the damage may be back-charged for the cost of the repairs. These charges may be deducted from any monies owed to the damaging contractor, by the homeowner. The choice for a contractor to repair the damages shall be at the sole discretion of the homeowner.

If no money is owed to the damaging contractor, said contractor shall pay the invoiced amount, from the homeowner, within seven business days. If prompt payment is not made, the homeowner may exercise all legal means to collect the requested monies.

The damaging contractor shall have no rights to lien the homeowner's property, for money retained to cover the repair of damages caused by the contractor. The homeowner may have the repairs made to their satisfaction.

The damaging contractor shall have the opportunity to quote a price for the repairs. The homeowner is under no obligation to engage the damaging contractor to make the repairs.

to individual products. These warranties should start with the date on the completion certificate. These simple forms take the guesswork out of warranty claims. They clearly establish the date all work was completed, inspected, and approved. This little piece of paper can make a big difference if you have a major malfunction or problem.

Many of the problems in remodeling are not caused by intentional deceit; they are caused by confusion. You are thinking one thing, and the contractor is thinking something else. You both have good intentions, but the conflict can get out of hand. Neither of you will want to give ground in the dispute when money is involved. With oral agreements there is no way to determine who is right. Written agreements eliminate the source of confusion. Each party knows exactly what he or she is expected to do and what he or she will be getting from the contractual relationship. It is also a good idea to include a clause about any damage that a contractor may cause during a job. Many problems arise when contractors damage personal property or the work of others.

Working with close friends can be the worst experience of your life. Business is business, and it can become a true threat to relationships. Friends don't want to insult each other; consequently, they avoid written contracts. Trust is not a factor, and the lack of a good contract can ruin your friendship. Financial disputes can turn into an all-out battle. The friend you golf with every week can become your worst enemy over a simple misunderstanding. Written contracts protect you and your friends.

Index

THE PROPHET

THE PROPHET

by
Kahlil Gibran

W

Wisehouse Classics

Kahlil Gibran

The Prophet

First published in 1923 by Alfred A. Knopf.

Published by Wisehouse Classics – Sweden

ISBN 978-91-7637-665-2

Wisehouse Classics is a Wisehouse Imprint.

© Wisehouse 2015 – Sweden

www.wisehouse-publishing.com

CONTENTS

THE COMING OF THE SHIP

ALMUSTAFA, the chosen and the beloved, who was a dawn unto his own day, had waited twelve years in the city of Orphalese for his ship that was to return and bear him back to the isle of his birth.

And in the twelfth year, on the seventh day of Ielool, the month of reaping, he climbed the hill without the city walls and looked seaward; and he beheld his ship coming with the mist.

Then the gates of his heart were flung open, and his joy flew far over the sea. And he closed his eyes and prayed in the silences of his soul.

∽

But as he descended the hill, a sadness came upon him, and he thought in his heart:

How shall I go in peace and without sorrow? Nay, not without a wound in the spirit shall I leave this city.

Long were the days of pain I have spent within its walls, and long were the nights of aloneness; and who can depart from his pain and his aloneness without regret?

Too many fragments of the spirit have I scattered in these streets, and too many are the children of my longing that walk naked among these hills, and I cannot withdraw from them without a burden and an ache.

It is not a garment I cast off this day, but a skin that I tear with my own hands.

Nor is it a thought I leave behind me, but a heart made sweet with hunger and with thirst.

∽

Yet I cannot tarry longer.

The sea that calls all things unto her calls me, and I must embark.

For to stay, though the hours burn in the night, is to freeze and crystallize and be bound in a mould.

Fain would I take with me all that is here. But how shall I?

A voice cannot carry the tongue and the lips that gave it wings. Alone must it seek the ether.

And alone and without his nest shall the eagle fly across the sun.

∽

Now when he reached the foot of the hill, he turned again towards the sea, and he saw his ship approaching the harbour, and upon her prow the mariners, the men of his own land.

∽

And his soul cried out to them, and he said:

Sons of my ancient mother, you riders of the tides,

How often have you sailed in my dreams. And now you come in my awakening, which is my deeper dream.

Ready am I to go, and my eagerness with sails full set awaits the wind.

Only another breath will I breathe in this still air, only another loving look cast backward,

And then I shall stand among you, a seafarer among seafarers.

And you, vast sea, sleeping mother,

Who alone are peace and freedom to the river and the stream,

Only another winding will this stream make, only another murmur in this glade,

And then I shall come to you, a boundless drop to a boundless ocean.

∼૭

And as he walked he saw from afar men and women leaving their fields and their vineyards and hastening towards the city gates.

And he heard their voices calling his name, and shouting from field to field telling one another of the coming of his ship.

∼૭

And he said to himself:

Shall the day of parting be the day of gathering?

And shall it be said that my eve was in truth my dawn?

And what shall I give unto him who has left his slough in midfurrow, or to him who has stopped the wheel of his winepress?

Shall my heart become a tree heavy-laden with fruit that I may gather and give unto them?

And shall my desires flow like a fountain that I may fill their cups?

Am I a harp that the hand of the mighty may touch me, or a flute that his breath may pass through me?

A seeker of silences am I, and what treasure have I found in silences that I may dispense with confidence?

If this is my day of harvest, in what fields have I sowed the seed, and in what unremembered seasons?

If this indeed be the hour in which I lift up my lantern, it is not my flame that shall burn therein.

Empty and dark shall I raise my lantern, And the guardian of the night shall fill it with oil and he shall light it also.

∼૭

These things he said in words. But much in his heart remained unsaid. For he himself could not speak his deeper secret.

~◦

And when he entered into the city all the people came to meet him, and they were crying out to him as with one voice.

And the elders of the city stood forth and said:

Go not yet away from us.

A noontide have you been in our twilight, and your youth has given us dreams to dream.

No stranger are you among us, nor a guest, but our son and our dearly beloved.

Suffer not yet our eyes to hunger for your face.

~◦

And the priests and the priestesses said unto him:

Let not the waves of the sea separate us now, and the years you have spent in our midst become a memory.

You have walked among us a spirit, and your shadow has been a light upon our faces.

Much have we loved you. But speechless was our love, and with veils has it been veiled.

Yet now it cries aloud unto you, and would stand revealed before you.

And ever has it been that love knows not its own depth until the hour of separation.

~◦

And others came also and entreated him. But he answered them not. He only bent his head; and those who stood near saw his tears falling upon his breast.

And he and the people proceeded towards the great square before the temple.

And there came out of the sanctuary a woman whose name was Almitra. And she was a seeress.

And he looked upon her with exceeding tenderness, for it was she who had first sought and believed in him when he had been but a day in their city.

And she hailed him, saying:

Prophet of God, in quest of the uttermost, long have you searched the distances for your ship.

And now your ship has come, and you must needs go.

Deep is your longing for the land of your memories and the dwelling-place of your greater desires; and our love would not bind you nor our needs hold you.

Yet this we ask ere you leave us, that you speak to us and give us of your truth.

And we will give it unto our children, and they unto their children, and it shall not perish.

In your aloneness you have watched with our days, and in your wakefulness you have listened to the weeping and the laughter of our sleep.

Now therefore disclose us to ourselves, and tell us all that has been shown you of that which is between birth and death.

And he answered:

People of Orphalese, of what can I speak save of that which is even now moving within your souls?

LOVE

THEN said Almitra, Speak to us of Love.
And he raised his head and looked upon the people, and there fell a stillness upon them. And with a great voice he said:

When love beckons to you, follow him,

Though his ways are hard and steep.

And When his wings enfold you yield to him,

Though the sword hidden among his pinions may wound you.

And When he speaks to you believe in him,

Though his voice may shatter your dreams as the north wind lays waste the garden.

For even as love crowns you so shall he crucify you.

Even as he is for your growth so is he for your pruning.

Even as he ascends to your height and caresses your tenderest branches that quiver in the sun,

So shall he descend to your roots and shake them in their clinging to the earth.

Like sheaves of corn he gathers you unto himself.

He threshes you to make you naked.

He sifts you to free you from your husks.

He grinds you to whiteness.

He kneads you until you are pliant;

And then he assigns you to his sacred fire, that you may become sacred bread for God's sacred feast.

All these things shall love do unto you that you may know the secrets of your heart, and in that knowledge become a fragment of Life's heart.

But if in your fear you would seek only love's peace and love's pleasure,

Then it is better for you that you cover your nakedness and pass out of love's threshing-floor,

Into the seasonless world where you shall laugh, but not all of your laughter, and weep, but not all of your tears.

Love gives naught but itself and takes naught but from itself.

Love possesses not nor would it be possessed;

For love is sufficient unto love.

When you love you should not say, "God is in my heart," but rather, "I am in the heart of God."

And think not you can direct the course of love, for love, if it finds you worthy, directs your course.

Love has no other desire but to fulfill itself.

But if you love and must needs have desires, let these be your desires:

To melt and be like a running brook that sings its melody to the night.

To know the pain of too much tenderness.

To be wounded by your own understanding of love;

And to bleed willingly and joyfully.

To wake at dawn with a winged heart and give thanks for another day of loving;

To rest at the noon hour and meditate love's ecstasy;

To return home at eventide with gratitude;

And then to sleep with a prayer for the beloved in your heart and a song of praise upon your lips.

MARRIAGE

THEN Almitra spoke again and said, And what of Marriage, master?
And he answered saying:

You were born together, and together you shall be for evermore.

You shall be together when the white wings of death scatter your days.

Aye, you shall be together even in the silent memory of God.

But let there be spaces in your togetherness.

And let the winds of the heavens dance between you.

Love one another, but make not a bond of love:

Let it rather be a moving sea between the shores of your souls.

Fill each other's cup but drink not from one cup.

Give one another of your bread but eat not from the same loaf.

Sing and dance together and be joyous, but let each one of you be alone,

Even as the strings of a lute are alone though they quiver with the same music.

Give your hearts, but not into each other's keeping.

For only the hand of Life can contain your hearts.

And stand together yet not too near together:

For the pillars of the temple stand apart,

And the oak tree and the cypress grow not in each other's shadow.

CHILDREN

AND a woman who held a babe against her bosom said, Speak to us of
Children.

And he said:

Your children are not your children.

They are the sons and daughters of Life's longing for itself.

They come through you but not from you,

And though they are with you yet they belong not to you.

You may give them your love but not your thoughts,

For they have their own thoughts.

You may house their bodies but not their souls,

For their souls dwell in the house of to-morrow, which you cannot visit, not even in your dreams.

You may strive to be like them, but seek not to make them like you.

For life goes not backward nor tarries with yesterday.

You are the bows from which your children as living arrows are sent forth.

The archer sees the mark upon the path of the infinite, and He bends you with His might that His arrows may go swift and far.

Let your bending in the Archer's hand be for gladness;

For even as He loves the arrow that flies, so He loves also the bow that is stable.

— ❧ —

GIVING

THEN said a rich man, Speak to us of Giving.
And he answered:

You give but little when you give of your possessions.

It is when you give of yourself that you truly give.

For what are your possessions but things you keep and guard for fear you may need them to-morrow?

And to-morrow, what shall to-morrow bring to the over-prudent dog burying bones in the trackless sand as he follows the pilgrims to the holy city?

And what is fear of need but need itself?

Is not dread of thirst when your well is full, the thirst that is unquenchable?

There are those who give little of the much which they have – and they give it for recognition and their hidden desire makes their gifts unwholesome.

And there are those who have little and give it all.

These are the believers in life and the bounty of life, and their coffer is never empty.

There are those who give with joy, and that joy is their reward.

And there are those who give with pain, and that pain is their baptism.

And there are those who give and know not pain in giving, nor do they seek joy, nor give with mindfulness of virtue;

They give as in yonder valley the myrtle breathes its fragrance into space.

Through the hands of such as these God speaks, and from behind their eyes He smiles upon the earth.

IT is well to give when asked, but it is better to give unasked, through understanding;

And to the open-handed the search for one who shall receive is joy greater than giving.

And is there aught you would withhold?

All you have shall some day be given;

Therefore, give now, that the season of giving may be yours and not your inheritors'.

~

You often say, "I would give, but only to the deserving."

The trees in your orchard say not so, nor the flocks in your pasture.

They give that they may live, for to withhold is to perish.

Surely he who is worthy to receive his days and his nights is worthy of all else from you.

And he who has deserved to drink from the ocean of life deserves to fill his cup from your little stream.

And what desert greater shall there be, than that which lies in the courage and the confidence, nay the charity, of receiving?

And who are you that men should rend their bosom and unveil their pride, that you may see their worth naked and their pride unabashed?

See first that you yourself deserve to be a giver, and an instrument of giving.

For in truth it is life that gives unto life-while you, who deem yourself a giver, are but a witness.

~

And you receivers – and you are all receivers – assume no weight of gratitude, lest you lay a yoke upon yourself and upon him who gives.

Rather rise together with the giver on his gifts as on wings;

For to be overmindful of your debt is to doubt his generosity who has the free-hearted earth for mother, and God for father.

~

EATING AND DRINKING

THEN an old man, a keeper of an inn, said, Speak to us of Eating and Drinking.

And he said:

Would that you could live on the fragrance of the earth, and like an air plant be sustained by the light.

But since you must kill to eat, and rob the newly born of its mother's milk to quench your thirst, let it then be an act of worship,

And let your board stand an altar on which the pure and the innocent of forest and plain are sacrificed for that which is purer and still more innocent in man.

When you kill a beast say to him in your heart:

"By the same power that slays you, I too am slain; and I too shall be consumed.

For the law that delivered you into my hand shall deliver me into a mightier hand.

Your blood and my blood is naught but the sap that feeds the tree of heaven."

And when you crush an apple with your teeth, say to it in your heart:

"Your seeds shall live in my body,

And the buds of your to-morrow shall blossom in my heart,

And your fragrance shall be my breath,

And together we shall rejoice through all the seasons."

And in the autumn, when you gather the grapes of your vineyards for the winepress, say in your heart:

"I too am a vineyard, and my fruit shall be gathered for the winepress,

And like new wine I shall be kept in eternal vessels."

And in winter, when you draw the wine, let there be in your heart a song for each cup;

And let there be in the song a remembrance for the autumn days, and for the vineyard, and for the winepress.

WORK

THEN a ploughman said, Speak to us of Work.
And he answered, saying:

You work that you may keep pace with the earth and the soul of the earth.

For to be idle is to become a stranger unto the seasons, and to step out of life's procession that marches in majesty and proud submission towards the infinite.

When you work you are a flute through whose heart the whispering of the hours turns to music.

Which of you would be a reed, dumb and silent, when all else sings together in unison?

Always you have been told that work is a curse and labour a misfortune.

But I say to you that when you work you fulfill a part of earth's furthest dream, assigned to you when that dream was born,

And in keeping yourself with labour you are in truth loving life,

And to love life through labour is to be intimate with life's inmost secret.

But if you in your pain call birth an affliction and the support of the flesh a curse written upon your brow, then I answer that naught but the sweat of your brow shall wash away that which is written.

You have been told also that life is darkness, and in your weariness you echo what was said by the weary.

And I say that life is indeed darkness save when there is urge,

And all urge is blind save when there is knowledge.

And all knowledge is vain save when there is work,

And all work is empty save when there is love;

And when you work with love you bind your self to yourself, and to one another, and to God.

And what is it to work with love?

It is to weave the cloth with threads drawn from your heart, even as if your beloved were to wear that cloth.

It is to build a house with affection, even as if your beloved were to dwell in that house.

It is to sow seeds with tenderness and reap the harvest with joy, even as if your beloved were to eat the fruit.

It is to charge all things you fashion with a breath of your own spirit,

And to know that all the blessed dead are standing about you and watching.

～

Often have I heard you say, as if speaking in sleep, "He who works in marble, and finds the shape of his own soul in the stone, is nobler than he who ploughs the soil.

And he who seizes the rainbow to lay it on a cloth in the likeness of man, is more than he who makes the sandals for our feet."

But I say, not in sleep, but in the overwakefulness of noontide, that the wind speaks not more sweetly to the giant oaks than to the least of all the blades of grass;

And he alone is great who turns the voice of the wind into a song made sweeter by his own loving.

～

Work is love made visible. And if you cannot work with love but only with distaste, it is better that you should leave your work and sit at the gate of the temple and take alms of those who work with joy.

For if you bake bread with indifference, you bake a bitter bread that feeds but half man's hunger.

And if you grudge the crushing of the grapes, your grudge distills a poison in the wine.

And if you sing though as angels, and love not the singing, you muffle man's ears to the voices of the day and the voices of the night.

～

JOY AND SORROW

THEN a woman said, Speak to us of Joy and Sorrow.
And he answered:

Your joy is your sorrow unmasked.

And the selfsame well from which your laughter rises was oftentimes filled with your tears.

And how else can it be?

The deeper that sorrow carves into your being, the more joy you can contain.

Is not the cup that holds your wine the very cup that was burned in the potter's oven?

And is not the lute that soothes your spirit the very wood that was hollowed with knives?

When you are joyous, look deep into your heart and you shall find it is only that which has given you sorrow that is giving you joy.

When you are sorrowful, look again in your heart, and you shall see that in truth you are weeping for that which has been your delight.

Some of you say, "Joy is greater than sorrow," and others say, "Nay, sorrow is the greater."

But I say unto you, they are inseparable.

Together they come, and when one sits alone with you at your board, remember that the other is asleep upon your bed.

～

Verily you are suspended like scales between your sorrow and your joy.

Only when you are empty are you at standstill and balanced.

When the treasure-keeper lifts you to weigh his gold and his silver, needs must your joy or your sorrow rise or fall.

～

HOUSES

THEN a mason came forth and said, Speak to us of Houses.
And he answered and said:

Build of your imaginings a bower in the wilderness ere you build a house within the city walls.

For even as you have home-comings in your twilight, so has the wanderer in you, the ever distant and alone.

Your house is your larger body.

It grows in the sun and sleeps in the stillness of the night; and it is not dreamless.

Does not your house dream? and dreaming, leave the city for grove or hilltop?

Would that I could gather your houses into my hand, and like a sower scatter them in forest and meadow.

Would the valleys were your streets, and the green paths your alleys, that you might seek one another through vineyards, and come with the fragrance of the earth in your garments.

But these things are not yet to be.

In their fear your forefathers gathered you too near together.

And that fear shall endure a little longer.

A little longer shall your city walls separate your hearths from your fields.

And tell me, people of Orphalese, what have you in these houses?

And what is it you guard with fastened doors?

Have you peace, the quiet urge that reveals your power?

Have you remembrances, the glimmering arches that span the summits of the mind?

Have you beauty, that leads the heart from things fashioned of wood and stone to the holy mountain?

Tell me, have you these in your houses?

Or have you only comfort, and the lust for comfort, that stealthy thing that enters the house a guest, and then becomes a host, and then a master?

Ay, and it becomes a tamer, and with hook and scourge makes puppets of your larger desires.

Though its hands are silken, its heart is of iron.

It lulls you to sleep only to stand by your bed and jeer at the dignity of the flesh.

It makes mock of your sound senses, and lays them in thistledown like fragile vessels.

Verily the lust for comfort murders the passion of the soul, and then walks grinning in the funeral.

But you, children of space, you restless in rest, you shall not be trapped nor tamed.

Your house shall be not an anchor but a mast.

It shall not be a glistening film that covers a wound, but an eyelid that guards the eye.

You shall not fold your wings that you may pass through doors, nor bend your heads that they strike not against a ceiling, nor fear to breathe lest walls should crack and fall down.

You shall not dwell in tombs made by the dead for the living.

And though of magnificence and splendour, your house shall not hold your secret nor shelter your longing.

For that which is boundless in you abides in the mansion of the sky, whose door is the morning mist, and whose windows are the songs and the silences of night.

CLOTHES

AND the weaver said, Speak to us of Clothes.
And he answered:

Your clothes conceal much of your beauty, yet they hide not the unbeautiful.

And though you seek in garments the freedom of privacy you may find in them a harness and a chain.

Would that you could meet the sun and the wind with more of your skin and less of your raiment.

For the breath of life is in the sunlight and the hand of life is in the wind.

Some of you say, "It is the north wind who has woven the clothes we wear."

And I say, Aye, it was the north wind,

But shame was his loom, and the softening of the sinews was his thread.

And when his work was done he laughed in the forest.

Forget not that modesty is for a shield against the eye of the unclean.

And when the unclean shall be no more, what were modesty but a fetter and a fouling of the mind?

And forget not that the earth delights to feel your bare feet and the winds long to play with your hair.

BUYING AND SELLING

AND a merchant said, Speak to us of Buying and Selling.
And he answered and said:

To you the earth yields her fruit, and you shall not want if you but know how to fill your hands.

It is in exchanging the gifts of the earth that you shall find abundance and be satisfied.

Yet unless the exchange be in love and kindly justice it will but lead some to greed and others to hunger.

When in the market-place you toilers of the sea and fields and vineyards meet the weavers and the potters and the gatherers of spices, –

Invoke then the master spirit of the earth, to come into your midst and sanctify the scales and the reckoning that weighs value against value.

And suffer not the barren-handed to take part in your transactions, who would sell their words for your labour.

To such men you should say:

"Come with us to the field, or go with our brothers to the sea and cast your net;

For the land and the sea shall be bountiful to you even as to us."

And if there come the singers and the dancers and the flute players, – buy of their gifts also.

For they too are gatherers of fruit and frankincense, and that which they bring, though fashioned of dreams, is raiment and food for your soul.

And before you leave the market-place, see that no one has gone his way with empty hands.

For the master spirit of the earth shall not sleep peacefully upon the wind till the needs of the least of you are satisfied.

CRIME AND PUNISHMENT

THEN one of the judges of the city stood forth and said, Speak to us of Crime and Punishment.

And he answered, saying:

It is when your spirit goes wandering upon the wind,

That you, alone and unguarded, commit a wrong unto others and therefore unto yourself.

And for that wrong committed must you knock and wait a while unheeded at the gate of the blessed.

Like the ocean is your god-self;

It remains for ever undefiled.

And like the ether it lifts but the winged.

Even like the sun is your god-self;

It knows not the ways of the mole nor seeks it the holes of the serpent.

But your god-self dwells not alone in your being.

Much in you is still man, and much in you is not yet man,

But a shapeless pigmy that walks asleep in the mist searching for its own awakening.

And of the man in you would I now speak.

For it is he and not your god-self nor the pigmy in the mist that knows crime and the punishment of crime.

Oftentimes have I heard you speak of one who commits a wrong as though he were not one of you, but a stranger unto you and an intruder upon your world.

But I say that even as the holy and the righteous cannot rise beyond the highest which is in each one of you,

So the wicked and the weak cannot fall lower than the lowest which is in you also.

And as a single leaf turns not yellow but with the silent knowledge of the whole tree,

So the wrong-doer cannot do wrong without the hidden will of you all.

Like a procession you walk together towards your god-self.

You are the way and the wayfarers.

And when one of you falls down he falls for those behind him, a caution against the stumbling stone.

Aye, and he falls for those ahead of him, who, though faster and surer of foot, yet removed not the stumbling stone.

And this also, though the word lie heavy upon your hearts:

The murdered is not unaccountable for his own murder,

And the robbed is not blameless in being robbed.

The righteous is not innocent of the deeds of the wicked,

And the white-handed is not clean in the doings of the felon.

Yea, the guilty is oftentimes the victim of the injured,

And still more often the condemned is the burden bearer for the guiltless and unblamed.

You cannot separate the just from the unjust and the good from the wicked;

For they stand together before the face of the sun even as the black thread and the white are woven together.

And when the black thread breaks, the weaver shall look into the whole cloth, and he shall examine the loom also.

If any of you would bring to judgment the unfaithful wife,

Let him also weigh the heart of her husband in scales, and measure his soul with measurements.

And let him who would lash the offender look unto the spirit of the offended.

And if any of you would punish in the name of righteousness and lay the axe unto the evil tree, let him see to its roots;

And verily he will find the roots of the good and the bad, the fruitful and the fruitless, all entwined together in the silent heart of the earth.

And you judges who would be just.

What judgment pronounce you upon him who though honest in the flesh yet is a thief in spirit?

What penalty lay you upon him who slays in the flesh yet is himself slain in the spirit?

And how prosecute you him who in action is a deceiver and an oppressor,

Yet who also is aggrieved and outraged?

~⁀

And how shall you punish those whose remorse is already greater than their misdeeds?

Is not remorse the justice which is administered by that very law which you would fain serve?

Yet you cannot lay remorse upon the innocent nor lift it from the heart of the guilty.

Unbidden shall it call in the night, that men may wake and gaze upon themselves.

And you who would understand justice, how shall you unless you look upon all deeds in the fullness of light?

Only then shall you know that the erect and the fallen are but one man standing in twilight between the night of his pigmy-self and the day of his god self,

And that the corner-stone of the temple is not higher than the lowest stone in its foundation.

—◌◌—

LAWS

Then a lawyer said, But what of our Laws, master?
And he answered:

You delight in laying down laws,

Yet you delight more in breaking them.

Like children playing by the ocean who build sand-towers with constancy and then destroy them with laughter.

But while you build your sand-towers the ocean brings more sand to the shore,

And when you destroy them the ocean laughs with you.

Verily the ocean laughs always with the innocent.

But what of those to whom life is not an ocean, and man-made laws are not sand-towers,

But to whom life is a rock, and the law a chisel with which they would carve it in their own likeness?

What of the cripple who hates dancers?

What of the ox who loves his yoke and deems the elk and deer of the forest stray and vagrant things?

What of the old serpent who cannot shed his skin, and calls all others naked and shameless?

And of him who comes early to the wedding feast, and when over-fed and tired goes his way saying that all feasts are violation and all feasters law-breakers?

What shall I say of these save that they too stand in the sunlight, but with their backs to the sun?

They see only their shadows, and their shadows are their laws.

And what is the sun to them but a caster of shadows?

And what is it to acknowledge the laws but to stoop down and trace their shadows upon the earth?

But you who walk facing the sun, what images drawn on the earth can hold you?

You who travel with the wind, what weather vane shall direct your course?

What man's law shall bind you if you break your yoke but upon no man's prison door?

What laws shall you fear if you dance but stumble against no man's iron chains?

And who is he that shall bring you to judgment if you tear off your garment yet leave it in no man's path?

People of Orphalese, you can muffle the drum, and you can loosen the strings of the lyre, but who shall command the skylark not to sing?

_ɔ∙ᴄ_

FREEDOM

AND an orator said, Speak to us of Freedom.
And he answered:

At the city gate and by your fireside I have seen you prostrate yourself and worship your own freedom,

Even as slaves humble themselves before a tyrant and praise him though he slays them.

Aye, in the grove of the temple and in the shadow of the citadel I have seen the freest among you wear their freedom as a yoke and a handcuff.

And my heart bled within me; for you can only be free when even the desire of seeking freedom becomes a harness to you, and when you cease to speak of freedom as a goal and a fulfillment.

You shall be free indeed when your days are not without a care nor your nights without a want and a grief,

But rather when these things girdle your life and yet you rise above them naked and unbound.

And how shall you rise beyond your days and nights unless you break the chains which you at the dawn of your understanding have fastened around your noon hour?

In truth that which you call freedom is the strongest of these chains, though its links glitter in the sun and dazzle your eyes.

∼ɔ

And what is it but fragments of your own self you would discard that you may become free?

If it is an unjust law you would abolish, that law was written with your own hand upon your own forehead.

You cannot erase it by burning your law books nor by washing the foreheads of your judges, though you pour the sea upon them.

And if it is a despot you would dethrone, see first that his throne erected within you is destroyed.

For how can a tyrant rule the free and the proud, but for a tyranny in their own freedom and a shame in their own pride?

And if it is a care you would cast off, that care has been chosen by you rather than imposed upon you.

And if it is a fear you would dispel, the seat of that fear is in your heart and not in the hand of the feared.

Verily all things move within your being in constant half embrace, the desired and the dreaded, the repugnant and the cherished, the pursued and that which you would escape.

These things move within you as lights and shadows in pairs that cling.

And when the shadow fades and is no more, the light that lingers becomes a shadow to another light.

And thus your freedom when it loses its fetters becomes itself the fetter of a greater freedom.

REASON AND PASSION

AND the priestess spoke again and said: Speak to us of Reason and Passion.

And he answered, saying:

Your soul is oftentimes a battlefield, upon which your reason and your judgment wage war against your passion and your appetite.

Would that I could be the peacemaker in your soul, that I might turn the discord and the rivalry of your elements into oneness and melody.

But how shall I, unless you yourselves be also the peacemakers, nay, the lovers of all your elements?

Your reason and your passion are the rudder and the sails of your seafaring soul.

If either your sails or your rudder be broken, you can but toss and drift, or else be held at a standstill in mid-seas.

For reason, ruling alone, is a force confining; and passion, unattended, is a flame that burns to its own destruction.

Therefore, let your soul exalt your reason to the height of passion, that it may sing;

And let it direct your passion with reason, that your passion may live through its own daily resurrection, and like the phoenix rise above its own ashes.

I would have you consider your judgment and your appetite even as you would two loved guests in your house.

Surely you would not honour one guest above the other; for he who is more mindful of one loses the love and the faith of both.

Among the hills, when you sit in the cool shade of the white poplars, sharing the peace and serenity of distant fields and meadows – then let your heart say in silence, "God rests in reason."

And when the storm comes, and the mighty wind shakes the forest, and thunder and lightning proclaim the majesty of the sky, – then let your heart say in awe, "God moves in passion."

And since you are a breath in God's sphere, and a leaf in God's forest, you too should rest in reason and move in passion.

─◌◌◌─

PAIN

AND a woman spoke, saying, Tell us of Pain.
And he said:

Your pain is the breaking of the shell that encloses your understanding.

Even as the stone of the fruit must break, that its heart may stand in the sun, so must you know pain.

And could you keep your heart in wonder at the daily miracles of your life, your pain would not seem less wondrous than your joy;

And you would accept the seasons of your heart, even as you have always accepted the seasons that pass over your fields.

And you would watch with serenity through the winters of your grief.

Much of your pain is self-chosen.

It is the bitter potion by which the physician within you heals your sick self.

Therefore, trust the physician, and drink his remedy in silence and tranquillity:

For his hand, though heavy and hard, is guided by the tender hand of the Unseen,

And the cup he brings, though it burn your lips, has been fashioned of the clay which the Potter has moistened with His own sacred tears.

─◌◌◌─

SELF-KNOWLEDGE

AND a man said, Speak to us of Self-Knowledge.

And he answered, saying:

Your hearts know in silence the secrets of the days and the nights.

But your ears thirst for the sound of your heart's knowledge.

You would know in words that which you have always known in thought.

You would touch with your fingers the naked body of your dreams.

And it is well you should.

The hidden well-spring of your soul must needs rise and run murmuring to the sea;

And the treasure of your infinite depths would be revealed to your eyes.

But let there be no scales to weigh your unknown treasure;

And seek not the depths of your knowledge with staff or sounding line.

For self is a sea boundless and measureless.

Say not, "I have found the truth," but rather, "I have found a truth."

Say not, "I have found the path of the soul." Say rather, "I have met the soul walking upon my path."

For the soul walks upon all paths.

The soul walks not upon a line, neither does it grow like a reed.

The soul unfolds itself, like a lotus of countless petals.

TEACHING

THEN said a teacher, Speak to us of Teaching.

And he said:

No man can reveal to you aught but that which already lies half asleep in the dawning of your knowledge.

The teacher who walks in the shadow of the temple, among his followers, gives not of his wisdom but rather of his faith and his lovingness.

If he is indeed wise he does not bid you enter the house of his wisdom, but rather leads you to the threshold of your own mind.

The astronomer may speak to you of his understanding of space, but he cannot give you his understanding.

The musician may sing to you of the rhythm which is in all space, but he cannot give you the ear which arrests the rhythm, nor the voice that echoes it.

And he who is versed in the science of numbers can tell of the regions of weight and measure, but he cannot conduct you thither.

For the vision of one man lends not its wings to another man.

And even as each one of you stands alone in God's knowledge, so must each one of you be alone in his knowledge of God and in his understanding of the earth.

FRIENDSHIP

AND a youth said, Speak to us of Friendship.
And he answered, saying:

Your friend is your needs answered.

He is your field which you sow with love and reap with thanksgiving.

And he is your board and your fireside.

For you come to him with your hunger, and you seek him for peace.

When your friend speaks his mind you fear not the "nay" in your own mind, nor do you withhold the "aye."

And when he is silent your heart ceases not to listen to his heart;

For without words, in friendship, all thoughts, all desires, all expectations are born and shared, with joy that is unclaimed.

when you part from your friend, you grieve not;

For that which you love most in him may be clearer in his absence, as the mountain to the climber is clearer from the plain.

And let there be no purpose in friendship save the deepening of the spirit.

For love that seeks aught but the disclosure of its own mystery is not love but a net cast forth: and only the unprofitable is caught.

And let your best be for your friend.

If he must know the ebb of your tide, let him know its flood also.

For what is your friend that you should seek him with hours to kill?

Seek him always with hours to live.

For it is his to fill your need, but not your emptiness.

And in the sweetness of friendship let there be laughter, and sharing of pleasures.

For in the dew of little things the heart finds its morning and is refreshed.

TALKING

A ND then a scholar said, Speak of Talking.

And he answered, saying:

You talk when you cease to be at peace with your thoughts;

And when you can no longer dwell in the solitude of your heart you live in your lips, and sound is a diversion and a pastime.

And in much of your talking, thinking is half murdered. For thought is a bird of space, that in a cage of words may indeed unfold its wings but cannot fly.

There are those among you who seek the talkative through fear of being alone.

The silence of aloneness reveals to their eyes their naked selves and they would escape.

And there are those who talk, and without knowledge or forethought reveal a truth which they themselves do not understand.

And there are those who have the truth within them, but they tell it not in words.

In the bosom of such as these the spirit dwells in rhythmic silence.

When you meet your friend on the roadside or in the market-place, let the spirit in you move your lips and direct your tongue.

Let the voice within your voice speak to the ear of his ear;

For his soul will keep the truth of your heart as the taste of the wine is remembered.

When the colour is forgotten and the vessel is no more.

TIME

AND an astronomer said, "Master, what of Time?"
And he answered:

You would measure time the measureless and the immeasurable.

You would adjust your conduct and even direct the course of your spirit according to hours and seasons.

Of time you would make a stream upon whose bank you would sit and watch its flowing.

Yet the timeless in you is aware of life's timelessness,

And knows that yesterday is but to-day's memory and to-morrow is to-day's dream.

And that which sings and contemplates in you is still dwelling within the bounds of that first moment which scattered the stars into space.

Who among you does not feel that his power to love is boundless?

And yet who does not feel that very love, though boundless, encompassed within the centre of his being, and moving not from love thought to love thought, nor from love deeds to other love deeds?

And is not time even as love is, undivided and paceless?

⁓

But if in your thought you must measure time into seasons, let each season encircle all the other seasons,

And let to-day embrace the past with remembrance and the future with longing.

⟡

GOOD AND EVIL

AND one of the elders of the city said, Speak to us of Good and Evil.
And he answered:

Of the good in you I can speak, but not of the evil.

For what is evil but good tortured by its own hunger and thirst?

Verily when good is hungry it seeks food even in dark caves, and when it thirsts it drinks even of dead waters.

You are good when you are one with yourself.

Yet when you are not one with yourself you are not evil.

For a divided house is not a den of thieves; it is only a divided house.

And a ship without rudder may wander aimlessly among perilous isles yet sink not to the bottom.

You are good when you strive to give of yourself.

Yet you are not evil when you seek gain for yourself.

For when you strive for gain you are but a root that clings to the earth and sucks at her breast.

Surely the fruit cannot say to the root, "Be like me, ripe and full and ever giving of your abundance."

For to the fruit giving is a need, as receiving is a need to the root.

~

You are good when you are fully awake in your speech.

Yet you are not evil when you sleep while your tongue staggers without purpose.

And even stumbling speech may strengthen a weak tongue.

~

You are good when you walk to your goal firmly and with bold steps.

Yet you are not evil when you go thither limping.

Even those who limp go not backward.

But you who are strong and swift, see that you do not limp before the lame, deeming it kindness.

~

You are good in countless ways, and you are not evil when you are not good,

You are only loitering and sluggard.

Pity that the stags cannot teach swiftness to the turtles.

~

IN your longing for your giant self lies your goodness: and that longing is in all of you.

But in some of you that longing is a torrent rushing with might to the sea, carrying the secrets of the hillsides and the songs of the forest.

And in others it is a flat stream that loses itself in angles and bends and lingers before it reaches the shore.

But let not him who longs much say to him who longs little, "Wherefore are you slow and halting?"

For the truly good ask not the naked, "Where is your garment?" nor the houseless, "What has befallen your house?"

~

PRAYER

THEN a priestess said, "Speak to us of Prayer."
And he answered, saying:

You pray in your distress and in your need; would that you might pray also in the fullness of your joy and in your days of abundance.

For what is prayer but the expansion of your self into the living ether?

And if it is for your comfort to pour your darkness into space, it is also for your delight to pour forth the dawning of your heart.

And if you cannot but weep when your soul summons you to prayer, she should spur you again and yet again, though weeping, until you shall come laughing.

When you pray you rise to meet in the air those who are praying at that very hour, and whom save in prayer you may not meet.

Therefore, let your visit to that temple invisible be for naught but ecstasy and sweet communion.

For if you should enter the temple for no other purpose than asking you shall not receive:

And if you should enter into it to humble yourself you shall not be lifted:

Or even if you should enter into it to beg for the good of others you shall not be heard.

It is enough that you enter the temple invisible.

～

I cannot teach you how to pray in words.

God listens not to your words save when He Himself utters them through your lips.

And I cannot teach you the prayer of the seas and the forests and the mountains.

But you who are born of the mountains and the forests and the seas can find their prayer in your heart,

And if you but listen in the stillness of the night you shall hear them saying in silence:

"Our God, who art our winged self, it is thy will in us that willeth.

"It is thy desire in us that desireth.

"It is thy urge in us that would turn our nights, which are thine, into days, which are thine also.

"We cannot ask thee for aught, for thou knowest our needs before they are born in us:

"Thou art our need; and in giving us more of thyself thou givest us all."

—∾∾—

PLEASURE

THEN a hermit, who visited the city once a year, came forth and said, Speak to us of Pleasure.

And he answered, saying:

Pleasure is a freedom-song,

But it is not freedom.

It is the blossoming of your desires,

But it is not their fruit.

It is a depth calling unto a height,

But it is not the deep nor the high.

It is the caged taking wing,

But it is not space encompassed.

Aye, in very truth, pleasure is a freedom-song.

And I fain would have you sing it with fullness of heart; yet I would not have you lose your hearts in the singing.

Some of your youth seek pleasure as if it were all, and they are judged and rebuked.

I would not judge nor rebuke them. I would have them seek.

For they shall find pleasure, but not her alone;

Seven are her sisters, and the least of them is more beautiful than pleasure.

Have you not heard of the man who was digging in the earth for roots and found a treasure?

∾

And some of your elders remember pleasures with regret like wrongs committed in drunkenness.

But regret is the beclouding of the mind and not its chastisement.

They should remember their pleasures with gratitude, as they would the harvest of a summer.

Yet if it comforts them to regret, let them be comforted.

∾

And there are among you those who are neither young to seek nor old to remember;

And in their fear of seeking and remembering they shun all pleasures, lest they neglect the spirit or offend against it.

But even in their foregoing is their pleasure.

And thus they too find a treasure though they dig for roots with quivering hands.

But tell me, who is he that can offend the spirit?

Shall the nightingale offend the stillness of the night, or the firefly the stars?

And shall your flame or your smoke burden the wind?

Think you the spirit is a still pool which you can trouble with a staff?

Oftentimes in denying yourself pleasure you do but store the desire in the recesses of your being.

Who knows but that which seems omitted to day, waits for to-morrow?

Even your body knows its heritage and its rightful need and will not be deceived.

And your body is the harp of your soul,

And it is yours to bring forth sweet music from it or confused sounds.

And now you ask in your heart, "How shall we distinguish that which is good in pleasure from that which is not good?"

Go to your fields and your gardens, and you shall learn that it is the pleasure of the bee to gather honey of the flower,

But it is also the pleasure of the flower to yield its honey to the bee.

For to the bee a flower is a fountain of life,

And to the flower a bee is a messenger of love,

And to both, bee and flower, the giving and the receiving of pleasure is a need and an ecstasy.

People of Orphalese, be in your pleasures like the flowers and the bees.

BEAUTY

AND a poet said, Speak to us of Beauty.
And he answered:

Where shall you seek beauty, and how shall you find her unless she herself be your way and your guide?

And how shall you speak of her except she be the weaver of your speech?

The aggrieved and the injured say, "Beauty is kind and gentle.

"Like a young mother half-shy of her own glory she walks among us."

And the passionate say, "Nay, beauty is a thing of might and dread.

"Like the tempest she shakes the earth beneath us and the sky above us."

~

The tired and the weary say, "Beauty is of soft whisperings.

"She speaks in our spirit.

"Her voice yields to our silences like a faint light that quivers in fear of the shadow."

But the restless say, "We have heard her shouting among the mountains,

"And with her cries came the sound of hoofs, and the beating of wings and the roaring of lions."

~

At night the watchmen of the city say, "Beauty shall rise with the dawn from the east."

And at noontide the toilers and the wayfarers say, "We have seen her leaning over the earth from the windows of the sunset."

~

In winter say the snow-bound, "She shall come with the spring leaping upon the hills."

And in the summer heat the reapers say, "We have seen her dancing with the autumn leaves, and we saw a drift of snow in her hair."

All these things have you said of beauty,

Yet in truth you spoke not of her but of needs unsatisfied,

And beauty is not a need but an ecstasy.

It is not a mouth thirsting nor an empty hand stretched forth,

But rather a heart inflamed and a soul enchanted.

It is not the image you would see nor the song you would hear,

But rather an image you see though you close your eyes and a song you hear though you shut your ears.

It is not the sap within the furrowed bark, nor a wing attached to a claw,

But rather a garden for ever in bloom and a flock of angels for ever in flight.

~

People of Orphalese, beauty is life when life unveils her holy face.

But you are life and you are the veil.

Beauty is eternity gazing at itself in a mirror.

But you are eternity and you are the mirror.

~

RELIGION

AND an old priest said, "Speak to us of Religion."
And he said:

Have I spoken this day of aught else?

Is not religion all deeds and all reflection,

And that which is neither deed nor reflection, but a wonder and a surprise ever springing in the soul, even while the hands hew the stone or tend the loom?

Who can separate his faith from his actions, or his belief from his occupations?

Who can spread his hours before him, saying,

"This for God and this for myself;

"This for my soul and this other for my body"?

All your hours are wings that beat through space from self to self.

He who wears his morality but as his best garment were better naked.

The wind and the sun will tear no holes in his skin.

And he who defines his conduct by ethics imprisons his song-bird in a cage.

The freest song comes not through bars and wires.

And he to whom worshipping is a window, to open but also to shut, has not yet visited the house of his soul whose windows are from dawn to dawn.

Your daily life is your temple and your religion.

Whenever you enter into it take with you your all.

Take the slough and the forge and the mallet and the lute,

The things you have fashioned in necessity or for delight.

For in reverie you cannot rise above your achievements nor fall lower than your failures.

And take with you all men:

For in adoration you cannot fly higher than their hopes nor humble yourself lower than their despair.

~

And if you would know God, be not therefore a solver of riddles.

Rather look about you and you shall see Him playing with your children.

And look into space; you shall see Him walking in the cloud, outstretching His arms in the lightning and descending in rain.

You shall see Him smiling in flowers, then rising and waving His hands in trees.

DEATH

THEN Almitra spoke, saying, "We would ask now of Death."
And he said:

You would know the secret of death.

But how shall you find it unless you seek it in the heart of life?

The owl whose night-bound eyes are blind unto the day cannot unveil the mystery of light.

If you would indeed behold the spirit of death, open your heart wide unto the body of life.

For life and death are one, even as the river and the sea are one.

IN the depth of your hopes and desires lies your silent knowledge of the beyond;

And like seeds dreaming beneath the snow your heart dreams of spring.

Trust the dreams, for in them is hidden the gate to eternity.

Your fear of death is but the trembling of the shepherd when he stands before the king whose hand is to be laid upon him in honour.

Is the shepherd not joyful beneath his trembling, that he shall wear the mark of the king?

Yet is he not more mindful of his trembling?

~

For what is it to die but to stand naked in the wind and to melt into the sun?

And what is it to cease breathing but to free the breath from its restless tides, that it may rise and expand and seek God unencumbered?

Only when you drink from the river of silence shall you indeed sing.

And when you have reached the mountain top, then you shall begin to climb.

And when the earth shall claim your limbs, then shall you truly dance.

THE FAREWELL

AND now it was evening.

And Almitra the seeress said, "Blessed be this day and this place and your spirit that has spoken."

And he answered,

Was it I who spoke?

Was I not also a listener?

Then he descended the steps of the Temple and all the people followed him.

And he reached his ship and stood upon the deck.

And facing the people again, he raised his voice and said:

People of Orphalese, the wind bids me leave you.

Less hasty am I than the wind, yet I must go.

We wanderers, ever seeking the lonelier way, begin no day where we have ended another day; and no sunrise finds us where sunset left us.

Even while the earth sleeps we travel.

We are the seeds of the tenacious plant, and it is in our ripeness and our fullness of heart that we are given to the wind and are scattered.

Brief were my days among you, and briefer still the words I have spoken.

But should my voice fade in your ears, and my love vanish in your memory, then I will come again,

And with a richer heart and lips more yielding to the spirit will I speak.

Yea, I shall return with the tide,

And though death may hide me, and the greater silence enfold me, yet again will I seek your understanding.

And not in vain will I seek.

If aught I have said is truth, that truth shall reveal itself in a clearer voice, and in words more kin to your thoughts.

~

I go with the wind, people of Orphalese, but not down into emptiness;

And if this day is not a fulfillment of your needs and my love, then let it be a promise till another day.

Man's needs change, but not his love, nor his desire that his love should satisfy his needs.

Know, therefore, that from the greater silence I shall return.

The mist that drifts away at dawn, leaving but dew in the fields, shall rise and gather into a cloud and then fall down in rain.

And not unlike the mist have I been.

In the stillness of the night I have walked in your streets, and my spirit has entered your houses,

And your heart-beats were in my heart, and your breath was upon my face, and I knew you all.

Aye, I knew your joy and your pain, and in your sleep your dreams were my dreams.

And oftentimes I was among you a lake among the mountains.

I mirrored the summits in you and the bending slopes, and even the passing flocks of your thoughts and your desires.

And to my silence came the laughter of your children in streams, and the longing of your youths in rivers.

And when they reached my depth the streams and the rivers ceased not yet to sing.

But sweeter still than laughter and greater than longing came to me.

It was the boundless in you;

The vast man in whom you are all but cells and sinews;

He in whose chant all your singing is but a soundless throbbing.

It is in the vast man that you are vast,

And in beholding him that I beheld you and loved you.

For what distances can love reach that are not in that vast sphere?

What visions, what expectations and what presumptions can outsoar that flight?

Like a giant oak tree covered with apple blossoms is the vast man in you.

His might binds you to the earth, his fragrance lifts you into space, and in his durability you are deathless.

You have been told that, even like a chain, you are as weak as your weakest link.

This is but half the truth.

You are also as strong as your strongest link.

To measure you by your smallest deed is to reckon the power of ocean by the frailty of its foam.

To judge you by your failures is to cast blame upon the seasons for their inconstancy.

～

Ay, you are like an ocean,

And though heavy-grounded ships await the tide upon your shores, yet, even like an ocean, you cannot hasten your tides.

And like the seasons you are also,

And though in your winter you deny your spring,

Yet spring, reposing within you, smiles in her drowsiness and is not offended.

Think not I say these things in order that you may say the one to the other,

"He praised us well.

"He saw but the good in us."

I only speak to you in words of that which you yourselves know in thought.

And what is word knowledge but a shadow of wordless knowledge?

Your thoughts and my words are waves from a sealed memory that keeps records of our yesterdays,

And of the ancient days when the earth knew not us nor herself,

And of nights when earth was upwrought with confusion.

～

Wise men have come to you to give you of their wisdom.

I came to take of your wisdom:

And behold I have found that which is greater than wisdom.

It is a flame spirit in you ever gathering more of itself,

While you, heedless of its expansion, bewail the withering of your days.

It is life in quest of life in bodies that fear the grave.

～

There are no graves here.

These mountains and plains are a cradle and a stepping-stone.

Whenever you pass by the field where you have laid your ancestors look well thereupon, and you shall see yourselves and your children dancing hand in hand.

Verily you often make merry without knowing.

～

Others have come to you to whom for golden promises made unto your faith you have given but riches and power and glory.

Less than a promise have I given, and yet more generous have you been to me.

You have given me my deeper thirsting after life.

Surely there is no greater gift to a man than that which turns all his aims into parching lips and all life into a fountain.

And in this lies my honour and my reward, –

That whenever I come to the fountain to drink I find the living water itself thirsty;

And it drinks me while I drink it.

Some of you have deemed me proud and over shy to receive gifts.

Too proud indeed am I to receive wages, but not gifts.

And though I have eaten berries among the hills when you would have had me sit at your board,

And slept in the portico of the temple when you would gladly have sheltered me,

Yet it was not your loving mindfulness of my days and my nights that made food sweet to my mouth and girdled my sleep with visions?

∽

For this I bless you most:

You give much and know not that you give at all.

Verily the kindness that gazes upon itself in a mirror turns to stone,

And a good deed that calls itself by tender names becomes the parent to a curse.

∽

And some of you have called me aloof, and drunk with my own aloneness,

And you have said,

"He holds council with the trees of the forest, but not with men.

"He sits alone on hill-tops and looks down upon our city."

True it is that I have climbed the hills and walked in remote places.

How could I have seen you save from a great height or a great distance?

How can one be indeed near unless he be far?

∽

And others among you called unto me, not in words, and they said:

"Stranger, stranger, lover of unreachable heights, why dwell you among the summits where eagles build their nests?

"Why seek you the unattainable?

42

"What storms would you trap in your net,

"And what vaporous birds do you hunt in the sky?

"Come and be one of us.

"Descend and appease your hunger with our bread and quench your thirst with our wine."

In the solitude of their souls they said these things;

But were their solitude deeper they would have known that I sought but the secret of your joy and your pain,

And I hunted only your larger selves that walk the sky.

But the hunter was also the hunted;

For many of my arrows left my bow only to seek my own breast.

And the flier was also the creeper;

For when my wings were spread in the sun their shadow upon the earth was a turtle.

And I the believer was also the doubter;

For often have I put my finger in my own wound that I might have the greater belief in you and the greater knowledge of you.

∾

And it is with this belief and this knowledge that I say,

You are not enclosed within your bodies, nor confined to houses or fields.

That which is you dwells above the mountain and roves with the wind.

It is not a thing that crawls into the sun for warmth or digs holes into darkness for safety,

But a thing free, a spirit that envelops the earth and moves in the ether.

∾

If these be vague words, then seek not to clear them.

Vague and nebulous is the beginning of all things, but not their end,

And I fain would have you remember me as a beginning.

Life, and all that lives, is conceived in the mist and not in the crystal.

And who knows but a crystal is mist in decay?

∾

This would I have you remember in remembering me:

That which seems most feeble and bewildered in you is the strongest and most determined.

Is it not your breath that has erected and hardened the structure of your bones?

And is it not a dream which none of you remember having dreamt, that built your city and fashioned all there is in it?

Could you but see the tides of that breath you would cease to see all else,

And if you could hear the whispering of the dream you would hear no other sound.

❧

But you do not see, nor do you hear, and it is well.

The veil that clouds your eyes shall be lifted by the hands that wove it,

And the clay that fills your ears shall be pierced by those fingers that kneaded it.

And you shall see.

And you shall hear.

Yet you shall not deplore having known blindness, nor regret having been deaf.

For in that day you shall know the hidden purposes in all things,

And you shall bless darkness as you would bless light.

❧

After saying these things, he looked about him, and he saw the pilot of his ship standing by the helm and gazing now at the full sails and now at the distance.

And he said:

Patient, over patient, is the captain of my ship.

The wind blows, and restless are the sails;

Even the rudder begs direction;

Yet quietly my captain awaits my silence.

And these my mariners, who have heard the choir of the greater sea, they too have heard me patiently.

Now they shall wait no longer.

I am ready.

The stream has reached the sea, and once more the great mother holds her son against her breast.

❧

Fare you well, people of Orphalese.

This day has ended.

It is closing upon us even as the water-lily upon its own to-morrow.

What was given us here we shall keep,

And if it suffices not, then again must we come together and together stretch our hands unto the giver.

Forget not that I shall come back to you.

A little while, and my longing shall gather dust and foam for another body.

A little while, a moment of rest upon the wind, and another woman shall bear me.

Farewell to you and the youth I have spent with you.

It was but yesterday we met in a dream.

You have sung to me in my aloneness, and I of your longings have built a tower in the sky.

But now our sleep has fled and our dream is over, and it is no longer dawn.

The noontide is upon us and our half waking has turned to fuller day, and we must part.

If in the twilight of memory, we should meet once more, we shall speak again together and you shall sing to me a deeper song.

And if our hands should meet in another dream we shall build another tower in the sky.

So saying he made a signal to the seamen, and straightaway they weighed anchor and cast the ship loose from its moorings, and they moved eastward.

And a cry came from the people as from a single heart, and it rose into the dusk and was carried out over the sea like a great trumpeting.

Only Almitra was silent, gazing after the ship until it had vanished into the mist.

And when all the people were dispersed she still stood alone upon the sea-wall, remembering in her heart his saying:

"A little while, a moment of rest upon the wind, and another woman shall bear me."

Manufactured by Amazon.ca
Bolton, ON

17146973R00028